CONTENTS

PART THREE: DESTINY ARRIVES

BOOK ONE OF THE ODYSSEY OF HOPE SERIES

RISING BEYOND HOPE

A MEMOIR OF GRIEF, LOSS, AND FAITH

MARVIN WILMES

KEY PUBLICATIONS

Published by Key Publications

Boone, Iowa 50036

www.marvinwilmes.com

Book Cover Design and Interior Formatting by 100Covers

Paperback ISBN: 979-8-9891613-1-7

Ebook ISBN: 979-8-9891613-4-8

Memoir disclaimer:

This work depicts actual events in the life of the author as truthfully as recollection permits and/or can be verified by research. Occasionally, dialogue consistent with the character or nature of the speaker has been added. All persons within are actual individuals; there are no composite characters. The names of some individuals have been changed to respect their privacy.

This memoir is designed to be used as a tool for personal reflection, a foundation for journaling, or as a springboard for discussion in a book club or any support group.

At the end of each chapter, there is a reflection and takeaways for you to explore. Journaling and reflection are gifts we can give ourselves as we set out on the journey of healing. Remember, your journey can begin with a single step, and be kind to yourself, as healing can sometimes come slowly through a process.

This memoir is a faith-based account; however, it is important to note that if you experience trauma and are finding it hard to cope, seek professional help. God does not intend for us to go it alone if we need further assistance in our emotional and mental health. Self-care should be at the top of our priorities.

DEDICATIONS

Dedicated to the memory of my mother, Peggy Wilmes, my Aunt Dee, Aunt Helen, and Chuck Ostermeier. They taught me the true meaning of rising beyond hope despite insurmountable losses.

To my wife, Lori, who has lovingly supported me through my many seasons of inspiration, loss, and writer's dreams with patient love and validation. She has provided me with the proper mixture of wisdom and caution when it comes to my creative soul's visions.

And to Deanne Welsh, my writing mentor, whom God provided to me after many years in the desert of going it alone. She has shown me the anchors to tie my work to as I go through the different seasons of my life.

My son, when you come to serve the Lord,
Stand in justice and fear,
Prepare yourself for trials.
Be sincere of heart and steadfast,
Incline your ear and receive the word of understanding,
Undisturbed in time of adversity.
Wait on God, with patience, cling to him,
Forsake him not,
Thus, will you be wise in all your ways.
Accept whatever befalls you,
When sorrowful, be steadfast,
And in crushing misfortune be patient,
For in fire gold and silver are tested,
And worthy people in the crucible of humiliation.
Trust God and God will help you.
Trust in Him, and He will direct your way.
Keep his fear and grow old therein.

You who fear the Lord, wait for His mercy,
Turn not away lest you fall.
You who fear the Lord, trust Him,
And your reward will not be lost.
You who fear the Lord,
Hope for good things.
For lasting joy and mercy.
You who fear the Lord, love Him,
And your hearts will be enlightened.
Study the generations long past and understand,
Has anyone hoped in the Lord and been disappointed?
Has anyone persevered in the command-
ments and been forsaken?
Has anyone called upon Him and been rebuffed?
Compassionate and merciful is the Lord,
He forgives sins, He saves in times of trouble,
And he is a protector to all who seek Him in truth.

Sirach 2: vs. 1-11

INTRODUCTION

"Even youths still faint and be weary, and young men shall fall exhausted; but they who wait upon the Lord shall renew their strength, they shall mount up with wings like eagles, they shall run and not be weary, they shall walk and not faint."

Isaiah 40, vs. 30-31

The past is behind you, and the future is ahead of you, so push forward and move on with your life.

Over a decade ago, the sign on the front of the neighborhood church startled me as I took the first tentative steps toward writing a memoir about the past. At one point in this journey, I shelved it because I asked myself, *Am I just stirring up old memories for no real purpose?*

Yet, a memory stirred in my soul.

"If you think this is bad, just wait."

The comment, delivered to me during an intensely trying time in my life, was meant to show empathy, but my spirit rejected it instead.

What this woman meant then, and what those words mean now in hindsight, are two different things. She challenged my entire belief system, and if I hadn't been careful, her words could easily have become a self-fulfilling prophecy.

I've always known that I have something to say. Still, a cancer diagnosis in 2010 and recovery led me to the deep well of emotion to write this memoir, which first appeared under the title *Beyond the Horizon: Crisis of Faith*, published in 2015.

Over the past decade, my vision for stories of faith, perseverance, and hope in the face of loss morphed into a retitled series of books under the umbrella of The Odyssey of Hope.

This series represents my witness to God's faithfulness in my life.

This memoir is designed to serve as a tool for personal reflection, a foundation for journaling, or a springboard for discussion in a book club or other support group.

Following each chapter, there is a reflection to guide discussion or journaling.

Journaling and reflection are gifts we can give ourselves as we embark on the journey of healing. Remember, your journey can begin with a single step, and be kind to yourself, as healing can sometimes come slowly through a process.

Have you ever been in situations that seem beyond hope, and if so, have you asked yourself how to overcome the despair that threatens to overtake you?

This first installment has always been "the book I am supposed to write," not as a puffed-up, prideful testament to who I am, but as a humble servant's witness to God's grace. It's not about me. I am only the messenger.

I began my journey anew as a cancer survivor in 2013, as I realized I was being called to write a story I never believed I could deliver with honesty. The first edition of *Beyond the Horizon, A Memoir* was published in January 2015 and made a big splash in my native land of northwestern Missouri.

God had authored this book simply by leading me through the passing phases of a lifetime. I will be the first to admit that there were times I was less than worthy of the task. Yet God works in mysterious ways. Many times, I opted to captain my own ship, but I am grateful for the times God granted me the grace to turn the wheel over to him.

In the sermon on the Mount, Jesus said, "*Blessed are they who mourn, for they will be comforted.*" **(Matthew 5:4.)**

Are you one who mourns?

Have you experienced a loss that at times seems insurmountable, the loss of a loved one, a cherished dream, a relationship, a job, a business venture, health, or finances? Have you lost your trust in God's providence? Maybe you are even angry with God. If so, you are not alone.

Nor are you beyond hope.

Hope must be our life-saving anchor in this life. Without hope, there can be no faith.

God seeks to comfort those who mourn, to help them move past their pain, and to enable them to move on with their lives. There is a proper process of grieving, of "putting away," and of taking on a powerful force of forgiveness and insight into our purpose in life.

In sharing my story, I intend to share specific periods in my faith journey as a wandering Catholic out of and back into the fullness and richness of the faith, experiencing a dramatic experience of discovery of who Jesus Christ really is at the age of 21 and developing a personal relationship with Jesus Christ, not understanding that my faith journey would lead to a second dramatic encounter at the age of 60.

I have always been Catholic, never actually leaving the church, still guided by the Holy Trinity, but not always practicing.

Many cradle Catholics today have fallen away, and from outside the church, many criticize and misunderstand the Catholic Church in this modern age.

This memoir series encompasses my spiritual journey. Like any work of art, it has evolved over the years into its current form.

This is not necessarily a denominational work. You do not have to be Catholic to gain inspiration from this story. In fact, in the spirit of Christian unity, it is not my desire to push away members of any denomination, but to witness how Jesus has given me the command to evangelize anyone who is seeking his offer of mercy and salvation, regardless of their faith of origin or their view of the Catholic religion.

We are all Christians. And if you haven't yet surrendered your life to Christ, maybe it's because you don't feel worthy.

I believe God will take you wherever you are on your path in life; you must ask Him, which involves surrender. Have you heard Him knocking at your door lately? Maybe God moved you to pick up this book, or someone gifted it to you.

I simply ask you to walk with me for a time. This memoir series is not about me. It is about the journey we all walk on this earth, day by day, step by step. None of us is perfect. We all have our struggles.

And grief sometimes blocks our road to redemption; we are all in need of healing in this area, whether we recognize it or not.

I recently reflected on a Scripture reading that magnifies God's faithfulness to us, even as we are constantly reminded to be faithful to God.

We are the ones most apt to turn our backs on God, but he will never turn his back on us and will always take us back, as evidenced by the Parable of the Prodigal Son.

All heaven will praise your great wonders, Lord; myriads of angels will praise you for your faithfulness.

For who in all of heaven can compare with the Lord? What mightiest angel is anything like the Lord?

The highest angelic powers stand in awe of God. He is far more awesome than all who surround his throne.

O Lord God of Heaven's Armies! Where is there anyone as mighty as you, O Lord? You are entirely faithful.

Psalm 89:5-8 NLT

I desire to give you hope despite experiences of loss, failure, or grief. I hope my words will help lead you along a path of rising above circumstances with the spirit born of an overcomer surrendered to God's will.

Let me share with you the part about being surrendered to God's will was not an easy one for me as I'm sure it is not for many of you, but Jesus has words of hope for you.

Jesus was a master storyteller himself, and He used parables to teach His followers.

We all have different gifts. He gave me the gift of writing for a purpose, and it has taken me a lifetime to realize how to fulfill that purpose. I will never personally know the souls who will be inspired and touched by my story, but God knows who you are.

For me, that is enough.

I cannot separate my experiences of the past with what God has taught me over the years. My past has been the rich field of discovery and none of us realize how the different seasons of our lives will ultimately shape our future.

I cannot believe that life is a random series of events. I've seen too many God winks, signal graces, or spiritual coincidences in my life to believe in relativism or randomness, but God has provided all men and women a free will to exercise as we wish.

We always have a choice to make, a crossroads to ponder, or an obstacle to overcome, even our own sin.

Through it all, God loves each one of us and calls us to do the same. With that love He also offers his mercy. So why is life so chaotic at times, and how can God allow bad things to happen to good people?

I believe God created a natural process for all of us to go through in overcoming life's many challenges. As I am the clay pot that the master potter works with to produce such an imperfect work of art, I am here to share my own story of processing life's events from the scattered remnants of the past into golden truths of the future.

We are all on a journey and through that journey we are molded into who we are today through a process.

Since 1978, God inspired me, prodded me, and allowed me to fail many times through many rough drafts of fiction and truth.

Ultimately, He worked life's circumstances to teach me about His power, wisdom, mercy, and grace. He asked me to tell my stories of loss and victories to ultimately minister to those suffering under the cross of grief.

My hope is you will learn, just as I have, that the important things are not what we see directly in the natural realm of this earthly life, which is temporal, but rather what we see in the truth that lies just beyond the horizon of eternity.

You can rise beyond hope.

PART ONE

THE EARLY YEARS

"All I have seen teaches me to trust the Creator for all I have not seen."

Ralph Waldo Emerson

CHAPTER ONE
A Cocoon of Innocence

"And he told them many things in parables, saying, 'A sower went out to sow. And as he sowed, some seeds fell along the path, and the birds came and devoured them. Other seeds fell on rocky ground, where they had not much soil, and immediately they sprang up, since they had no depth of soil, but when the sun rose, they were scorched; and since they had no root, they withered away. Other seeds fell among thorns, and the thorns grew up and choked them. Other seed fell on good soil and brought forth grain, some hundredfold, some sixty, some thirty. He who has ears, let him hear.'"

MATTHEW 13 VS 3-9

As 1963 began, the country felt wrapped in a cocoon of innocence—soft, untroubled, confident. My world was even smaller and safer: seven simple years on a farm, under the watchful eyes of my father's three youngest brothers, Phil, Tom, and Ken. They weren't just uncles; they were "older brothers" that time gifted me. Aunt Dee—three years older than me and the youngest of my grandparents' remarkable sixteen—completed our lively tribe.

Uncle Phil taught me how to climb fences before I could pronounce the word "balance." I still see his big hands like bookends on either side of me, guiding me rung by rung. "Come on, Marvin, easy does it," he said, voice steady as a fencepost. "You've got it."

"Don't let me fall," I pleaded.

Phil chuckled. "Don't worry about that. I'll catch you."

And somehow, with him below, the sky never felt too high.

Uncle Tom was the daredevil. He'd roar down the gravel road in his blue Chevy convertible, the wind needling my cheeks while he yelled into the horizon. He'd light cherry bombs, flick them into the ditch, and laugh as they cracked the silence of Missouri fields. "Oh yeah!" he hollered into the wind, while I pressed my invisible brake on the passenger side—half terrified, half grinning, fully alive.

Every year, I tested myself against the same dragon: The Wizard of Oz on our old Sylvania blackandwhite. The rabbit ears wore a halo of aluminum foil; the screen hummed like a beehive. And then—whoosh! —The Wicked Witch of the West bloomed from smoke, and my courage evaporated.

One Saturday night, Tom came to babysit.

"Can we watch The Wizard of Oz?" I pleaded.

"I guess so," he said, "though I've seen it about a hundred times."

The minute the witch appeared, I bolted to my room and slid under the bed, boards and dust bunnies pressing into my back. Tom leaned in the doorway, exasperated and amused. "Why are you so scared? You've seen this before. Come on out of there."

"No, I don't like her."

"So why did you want to watch?"

I couldn't answer that question. I only knew that some things are so scary you can't stop looking. The movie pulled me back year after year, and the fear arrived right on cue.

Even then, I sensed it: a seam of darkness stitched beneath the bright fabric of the world. Witches I could handle; needles, I could not. At the doctor's office, the nurse turned witchlike—sharp, efficient, merciless—her needle a broomstick. I'd leave dotted in welts and bruises, my bravery leaking out in pinpricks. So, when Aunt Dee and Uncle Ken took me for my smallpox vaccination, dread rode shotgun.

"You 'fraidy cat, you ain't gonna be afraid of no needle," Dee teased, loving her "big sister" role.

"You don't know this nurse," I said. "She's mean, and her shots always hurt."

"I'll get mine first," Dee declared, rolling up her sleeve like a knight lifting a visor. "See? Nothing to worry about." I watched. She flinched once. "Just a pinprick," she announced.

I stepped up, opened my sleeve, shut my eyes tight enough to see stars.

"There, all done," the nurse said.

I cracked one eye. She was smiling—and I wasn't crying. For once, courage didn't feel like a performance. It felt like a quiet surprise.

Strong Family Roots

I was born Marvin LeRoy Wilmes, the third grandchild of George and Gertrude Wilmes—farm folk who took seriously the Lord's call to be fruitful and multiply. My father, Alfred Francis Wilmes, was the second oldest of sixteen, raised in a world where chores came before dawn and ended after dark. My mother, Margaret Ellen "Peggy"

Tuttle Wilmes, was an only child, though technically the middle of three. Her brothers died at birth, a sorrow that left her both treasured and solitary. Those two currents, my father's bustling clan and my mother's quiet singularity, met in our house and made a steady river.

Mom's mother, Naomi Miller Tuttle, was a born teacher—trained in the one-room schoolhouses of yesteryear, as comfortable with primers and chalk as with bread dough and hymns. Mother and daughter were closest when school ruled the calendar; letting go, when Mom became a woman, proved harder for Naomi. In her heart, Mom was always "her little girl." Few recognized Naomi's steel—gentle, intentional, and unyielding in the ways that mattered. But time would.

Grandpa Roy cast a long, easy shadow. Oldest of six, he'd been nine when his mother died of tuberculosis. An Irish patriarch took him and four siblings in; a relative adopted the youngest. Their father vanished into silence. In that generation, people didn't investigate grief; they endured it. Roy assumed desertion and learned to shoulder the heavy cross of abandonment.

He worked as a hired hand, moving his family from farm to farm, sometimes every year. He survived the Great Depression, tilled reluctant soil, and wore his shyness like a coat that fit. He was a devout Catholic who married a woman whose faith ran more in devotion than in doctrine—Naomi's love poured out in the way she taught children.

They wed in lean years, and lean years left their mark—later, even in comfort, they braced for the next downturn as if it were already pulling into the driveway. In the early 1940s, they bought her father's farm and took root in Naomi's childhood ground near

Parnell, Missouri, in the rolling folds of Worth County. That's where Mom—Peggy—grew up.

Time pressed forward. Farming modernized faster than Roy wanted, and in 1958, Missouri shuttered its one-room schoolhouses. Naomi, never one to be outpaced, earned her master's degree at Northwest Missouri State Teachers College in Maryville. When she landed a job at Southeast Elementary in Kansas City, she was thrilled—and then heartbroken. The farm, sold to a neighbor on a rent-to-own agreement, finally slipped away. Mom remembered holding her mother that day, both learning how to let go of the ground that had held them.

Roy followed Naomi to the city, starting fresh as a school bus driver and discovering he liked the rowdy hopefulness of kids. He moved on to custodial work at Platte Hills Junior High and, somehow, found his calling there—steady, kind, the sort of man boys measured themselves against without knowing.

He took the three-to-eleven shift; Naomi taught nine months a year. They made new friends. We were only two hours away. On weekends, they'd pull into our farm, and the "west room" became their motel. Other times, we'd head to Parkville, the drive stitched together with fields and stories. For my brother Vincent and me, "going to Grandma and Grandpa's" meant safety with a front porch.

That move gave Roy and Naomi a new lease on life and the stability they had once prayed for. Roy became proof that a person can climb—slowly, stubbornly—from rags to comfortable means, if he keeps showing up. Maybe that's where my fenceclimbing started: with men who stood below and said, Easy does it, you've got it—and meant it.

The rooftop test of trust

On my father's side, Grandpa George was the storyteller. My grandfather could turn a slow afternoon into a frontrow seat at the theater. He'd lean back, cock an eyebrow, and conduct the room with his right hand—two fingers gone to a farming accident, the stump flashing like a badge of survival—as he spun gossip about "old codger" neighbors and the latest troubles of the world. His voice made fences creak, tractors cough, and men laugh in your ear. I believed everything he said, not because he insisted on it, but because he seemed to belong to the weather and the land themselves.

One summer day, Grandpa called down to me from the roof of the half-built bathroom addition like a ringmaster inviting a lion cub into the ring. He grinned wide, palm out. I climbed the ladder rung by rung, grip slick with excitement, and when I caught his hand, he lifted me in a single, easy pull that made my stomach swoop. Standing up there beside him, wind in my hair, shingles warm under my shoes, I felt like a big little man—safe because he said I was.

Gertrude, the whitehaired general

Grandma Gertrude's hair was white for as long as my memory stretches, a crown earned the hard way. Sixteen births, including the fraternal twins—Geri and Jerry—would do that to a woman. Their marriage ran on the gears of its time: he provided and protected; she kept the house marching in formation and dinner steaming on the table. But if Grandpa was the headline, Grandma was the editor.

Her voice flew two octaves above the daily commotion, not sharp, just strong enough to be heard over a chorus of children. She surrendered much of her social life to the swarm she loved, and I never heard her call it a sacrifice. She prayed us through those years—rosary beads slipping through her fingers, whispering names and needs into the quiet. I didn't understand the faith then, not really. But it laid roots beneath me, hidden and alive, waiting to hold when I needed them most. The answers didn't always come when she asked for them; some arrived decades later, like mail forwarded by heaven.

Nephew or "lil' brother?

Being the younger Wilmes among a pack of seasoned aunts and uncles fit me like a hand-me-down sweater that somehow looked tailor-made. I trailed them on errands, chores, joyrides, whatever excuse got me within their orbit. They were my early definition of capable and kind, and I wore their confidence like armor.

Our home was a mile from my grandparents, but it might as well have been inside their circle of warmth. Those first seven years shimmered with stability—faith at the center, family around it. I didn't know my parents started with ninety dollars a month and grit; all I knew was we belonged to each other.

Cousin Elmer would toddle over from down the way, and we'd scoop him up for church. Then my brother arrived. At three years old, I felt my world tilt. The visiting ward at St. Francis smelled like soap and something metallic; the floors shone so bright I didn't want to scuff them. Mom placed that tightswaddled bundle in my lap, proud and glowing. I held him as he might break, jealousy pricking at me even as wonder filled my chest. Mom's happiness tugged me toward my own. If she smiled, I could learn to smile too.

The White Stallion and Blue Goose

Grandpa kept dairy cows, hogs, and a few horses—a kingdom to a boy. One afternoon, Aunt Dee boosted me onto a white stallion that decided to test the limits of both of us. He launched like we'd heard a gun at the Kentucky Derby. "Hang on!" Aunt Dee shouted, her voice shredding the air behind me. My fingers locked in the mane; my breath came in fast bursts; the world blurred into a stream of pasture and sky. Fear and joy braided into something fierce, and I discovered a muscle I didn't know I had: the will to hold on.

When the younger aunts and uncles learned to drive, the training wheels looked like a dented, bus-like contraption caked in blue paint. We called it Blue Goose. I'd scramble beside Aunt Geri, who shifted like she was wrestling a stubborn bull. "Hang tight, Marvin," she'd say, grinding a protest from the gearbox as she aimed us between the farm gate posts. "Do you even know what you're doing?" Aunt Dee would laugh from the passenger seat. "Not yet," Geri grinned, "but I will." And somehow, with a final cough, the Goose would lurch triumphantly.

Faith, schools, and long hopes

Grandpa George ran a simple playbook that still felt grand: sons to the field after eighth grade, daughters to Catholic boarding schools, everyone shaped by a structure bigger than themselves. My dad boarded in town at St. Patrick's Catholic School through eighth grade and looked up to Father Isadore as a star to navigate by. Then he went to the fields, where characters were plowed row by row.

George's sister, Genevieve Wilmes, took vows as a nun. His sister Rose married Grandma's brother Alfred. They had no children, but they carried quiet wisdom that made rooms gentler. Rose stood firm in God's will, cutting hair and spreading a softer gospel with her hands. Grandpa dreamed, almost dared heaven, to send a priest down our line. The answer didn't bloom in his lifetime, but Aunt Louise's grandson eventually stepped into the collar. Prayers aren't clocks; they're seeds. Some burst in spring. Others wait out a few winters.

Hay wagon adventure

Trust was the air I breathed among my uncles. One summer, I sat on the lowboy as they helped Dad stack fresh bales—Ken at the tractor, Phil balancing high, Tom and Dad tossing hay like they were building a golden wall.

I was safe by the wheel hub, but I wanted to stand tall like Phil. I rose, took a step, and the wagon bucked over a ditch. The world jolted. I flew forward. My mouth hit wood. Phil's hands snatched into the empty air. Warmth flooded my lips, and I spit out a tooth, stunned more by the shout of my father's anger than the pain itself.

"What's wrong with you?" Dad barked at Ken. "Who taught you to drive?" Ken absorbed it, silent.

Phil crouched by me. "You alright?" he asked, softer than the hay around us.

I couldn't answer. Guilt sat heavier than hurt. In my head, I kept repeating: It was my fault. I wanted to be big. Dad's voice gentled when he turned to me. "You okay, son?" I nodded and held up the tooth like a white flag. I walked to the house, leaving a dotted red line behind me, learning with each step that growing has a price.

In those early years, under the steady hands of George and Gertrude and a household stitched together by faith, I learned what provision feels like—quiet, reliable, present. I also learned the strange arithmetic of becoming: to reach for the next rung, you sometimes must lose your grip on the last. A tooth, a fear, a bit of pride always gives something better to take root. And in the spaces between loss and gain, prayers keep working, even when we can't hear them.

Reflections and Takeaways

- **The Power of Family Bonds:** The chapter underscores the profound impact of close family relationships, particularly the influence of mentors and role models within a family unit. Who in your own life provided that same sense of guidance and support?
- **Confronting Fear and Embracing Courage:** The anecdotes about facing fears, both big and small, highlight the importance of developing courage and resilience. How have you approached your own fears, and what strategies can you use to overcome them?
- **The Importance of Values and Legacy:** The chapter explores the family's history, emphasizing the values handed down through generations. It encourages you to reflect on the values that have shaped your life and the legacy you hope to leave behind.
- **Embracing Change and Growth:** The arrival of the author›s brother symbolizes the inevitable changes that occur throughout life. Growth often involves letting go of the old and embracing the new, even when it›s challenging.
- **The Enduring Power of Faith and Hope:** Even amidst difficulties, the importance of faith and prayer is emphasized. I encourage you to find strength and hope, particularly during times of uncertainty and adversity.

In essence, Chapter One serves as a potent reminder to cherish family connections, confront fears with courage, embrace change, and find strength in faith and hope, as we all navigate our own life's journeys.

What signposts in your youth guide you today, and who were your mentors? How have they positively or negatively influenced who you are today?

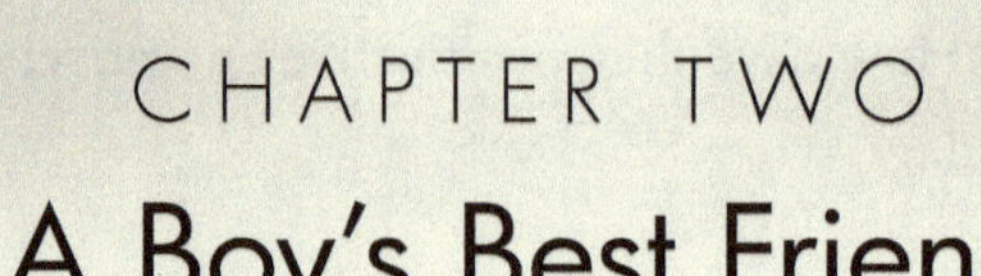

CHAPTER TWO
A Boy's Best Friend

"The dog was created specially for children. He is the god of frolic."

HENRY WARD BEECHER

"Out of the ground the LORD God formed every beast of the field and every bird of the sky and brought them to the man to see what he would call them; and whatever the man called a living creature, that was its name."

GENESIS 2: 19

Hope, in our house, wore work boots. It asked for change as often as it promised comfort. In 1963, it came to our kitchen table and nudged my father to let go—of the fields he knew, of the house that held my childhood, and of the nine years he'd worked beside my grandfather after two in the United States Marine Corps and a young marriage to my mother. Around the time his brother Raymond got engaged, a quiet restlessness in Dad began to take root, the kind that makes a man pace doorways and stare out windows.

On the day he decided, he looked older, as if the choice itself were a burden. He stood before my mother with his head bowed, lifted his sweat-damp cap, and brushed a palm over his flattop. When he finally met her eyes, his voice carried a tremor I would only later recognize as grief. "It's time to move on," he said. "I've had a good nine years, but it's time to do this on my own." My mother didn't say much—she rarely needed to. They had a way of speaking without words, a current of understanding I grew up trusting as love.

Dad started hunting for a place immediately, never one to linger on a goodbye. I wasn't so brave. I stared a long while at our one-story house, the tire swing by the tree, and buried my face in the fur of Tippie, our mixed-breed collie. That swing wouldn't hold me anymore. For the first time, loss had a shape I could name.

Moving day broke cold and bright, snow lacing the fields outside my grandparents' house. It was my last day at St. Patrick's, and I burrowed deeper under the covers when Uncle Ken shook my shoulder. "Go away," I mumbled. "I'm not going to school today."

He guided me downstairs anyway, where Grandma Gertrude waited—steadfast as an oak. "You will go to school," she said, not unkindly, but with a firmness that left no room for argument. "No playing hooky today."

"But Mama and Daddy are moving," I tried.

"Yes," Ken said, "and you'll join them after school." Traitor, I thought. You don't understand. I don't want to say goodbye.

The new farm was nearly twenty-five miles away, six miles west of Parnell, Missouri—population 250. My second-grade class would have twenty-five students. Awkward, I figured, but maybe joyful, too. Tippie and I would miss the old place, yet a new adventure beckoned. When my parents picked me up after school, I ran to my mother and wrapped my arms around her, bracing for the unknown. We reached the two-story farmhouse at dusk. Vincent and I tumbled out of the car and chased Tippie through the snow until my lungs burned with cold. And there it was—that settling in my chest. I was home again.

I had stepped out from the shadow of my aunts and uncles, from the steely eyed stares of the stern nuns at St. Patrick's—those women with eyes in the backs of their heads—and into the halls of Northeast Nodaway R-V Elementary in Parnell. I wanted to prove myself. A lanky Ravenwood kid seemed to measure me the way boys do, and I felt the heat of his jealousy, or maybe my own need to stand tall.

Our teacher, Mrs. B. K. Lewis, wore horn-rimmed glasses and a stare that could pin you to your seat. One afternoon, when she slipped out on an errand, I decided to put on a show—her voice, her stance, the whole routine—playing teacher to a room of giggling classmates. I didn't know she was a friend of my maternal grandmother. The door swung open mid-performance. The crack of her hand meeting my backside echoed louder than the laughter, and before my yelp faded, I was marching down to the principal's office. Freedom, I discovered, often came with borders—and consequences.

Our small school was a factory for legends. A frail woman lived down the lane with a cat tucked in her elbow; one recess she waved us over. "Cookies and milk?" she asked, gentle as a breeze. Fear did the rest. We ran, imagining the worst.

A classmate, Bob Welch, lived next door to her. He stoked the fire of fear—a black cauldron, he claimed, a soup pot for boiling little boys in. Later, my mother and grandmother told me the truth: she was as harmless as the kitten she held. Shame flushed through me, a lesson in how easily kindness can look like danger when you're young.

Sundays anchored us. St. Joseph's Catholic Church in Parnell felt small and serene next to the towering stone of Maryville's parish. We never questioned going—holy days, too. Father Andrew, elderly and peering through thick bifocals, seemed unable to find a smile, his patience as thin as candle smoke. The balance to that sternness came from stories like those told by my grandmother's half-aunt, Lena Logan. She never wore dentures, her tongue darting as she spoke, and once she took the wheel when her husband died of a heart attack beside her—she didn't know how to drive but somehow got them safely stopped. "Jesus saved me," she said. "All you have to do is holler, 'Jesus, save me,' and he will." He did for her, she promised. He would do the same for us.

In that first winter on the farm, I learned what it meant to be both afraid and brave—leaving the heroes of my childhood, testing new edges, and trusting that hope, even when it sounded like loss, might be pointing us home.

Holding on teaches you the weight of love; letting go teaches you its shape. When we moved into the new farmhouse, even the stairs felt like a novelty—two stories where we'd once had one, rooms echoing with the unfamiliar.

Tippie came with us, trotting circles in the yard as if mapping the borders of our new life. A week in, on a chill morning that glittered the fields, Dad asked, "Where's Tippie?"

Mom shook her head. "I don't know. I haven't seen him all morning."

By the time I got home from school, the absence had hardened into fact. "I'll look for him," I offered, and I did—behind the corncrib, along the fence line, down the rutted lane where the wind tugged my sleeve like a warning. Night fell, and no familiar bark cut the dark. I kept my face dry, not out of bravery, but because the sadness felt too big for tears.

On Saturday, my grandparents came. Grandpa Roy stood on the porch and squinted toward the horizon. "He probably headed home and got lost," he said, jaw tight, eyes fixed to the east—even though, in my boy-mind, Tippie's home was west. I didn't understand his direction then, only the grief tugging at his lip and the way he lingered in the doorway long after the grown-ups went inside. He was the last one to stop looking.

I remember, too, my father's arms circling my mother from behind, his chin on her shoulder—a quiet shelter I mistook as comfort for me alone.

Years later, Dad would tell me what I hadn't yet learned to see: Tippie had been "Grandpa's dog." With that truth, the map in my head redrew itself. Of course, Grandpa faced east; his homestead lay northeast of Parnell in the rolling hills of Worth County. That was the "home" Tippie knew.

Decades on, I let the mystery close gently. I came to believe Tippie did what loyal dogs do—he went home, the one beyond our finding, where all good dogs go. The move and Tippie's disappearance marked the opening of a season I wouldn't name until much later: 1963 was not just change; it was loss, learning to speak, trauma bending the edges of childhood until the picture no longer lay flat.

Trixie

Grief, my mother understood, can't be argued with—but it can be met. Not long after Tippie vanished, she drove Vincent and me to a tidy two-story building on the east side of Maryville. A middle-aged woman lifted a basket, and out sprang a blackandwhite terrier with a heartbeat for a tail. We knelt, and she licked our fingers like we'd been hers all along. "Trixie," we decided, and the name fit as snug as her paws in the crooks of our arms.

Trixie ran on pure joy. She chased our boots across the pasture and shadowed Dad as he made his rounds, a small sentinel keeping pace with the big work of a farm. With her came a widening of my world—days that reached beyond the familiar orbit of aunts and uncles, beyond the strict corridors of who I'd been.

Every childhood has its bend in the road, the place where innocence blinks and begins to see. Mine was just ahead.

Reflections and Takeaways from Chapter Two

This chapter captures a child's first apprenticeship in loss and belonging, set against a family's leap toward self-determination in rural Missouri in 1963. The opening metaphor, "Hope, in our house, wore work boots," anchors the piece in a working-class ethic where love is enacted through risk, labor, and quiet endurance. The author's father's decision to leave the security of the family farm and "do this on my own" carries both courage and grief; the scene of him brushing his flattop before speaking reads as a small, masculine liturgy of vulnerability. His mother's steady presence becomes the counterweight—love here is less spoken than practiced.

The move refracts through a child's eyes: the one-story house and tire swing recede; a two-story farmhouse becomes vast with possibility; snow and lung-stinging mark the body's record of change. School introduces a new moral perimeter—"Freedom… came with borders—and consequences"—as playacting authority collides with absolute authority. The neighborhood legend of the woman with the kitten lays bare how fear distorts perception; the boy's later shame is the hinge that turns toward empathy. In parallel, Catholic ritual offers constancy while stories like Aunt Lena's infuse stern faith with lived grace, sketching a community where severity and salvation co-exist.

Tippie's disappearance is the chapter's emotional fulcrum. What begins as a child's grief expands into a generational map of allegiance: only later do you learn Tippie was "Grandpa's dog," and the east-west correction redraws an inner compass. Home becomes less a place than a vector of loyalty. Accepting the unknowable—"where all good dogs go"—is both elegy and ethic: loss need not be solved to be honored. His mother's response—bringing Trixie into the family—models grief met with care, not denial. The dog becomes a conduit of renewed joy and a widened world.

Formally, the chapter braids crisp vignettes—kitchen-table leave-taking, playground bravado, parish ritual, the wind-tugged search—into a coherent emotional arc. Recurring motifs (work boots, borders, doorways, directions) guide the reader through shifting ground. The voice balances tenderness with restraint, hindsight with immediacy. By closing on "Every childhood has its bend in the road," the chapter identifies the moment innocence learns to see—and keeps going.

Key Takeaways

- Core theme: Self-reliance costs something—independence is purchased with grief, and love must change shape to endure.
- Re-mapping "home": East vs. west becomes a moral geography; belonging is directional, relational, and sometimes invisible until hindsight.
- Loss embodied: Tippie's disappearance teaches that love can pull in different directions—and that acceptance is a form of faith.
- Borders of freedom: The classroom episode reframes freedom as responsibility; authority is both external (teacher, church) and internal (conscience).
- Fear vs. empathy: The "witch" legend shows how stories can harm; later understanding cultivates compassion over suspicion.

- Faith in tension: Parish severity meets Aunt Lena's everyday miracle, presenting belief as both discipline and refuge.
- Craft insight: Vignettes plus motifs (work boots, thresholds, directions) braid memory into a clear narrative arc; the aphoristic line on holding/letting go crystallizes the chapter's ethic.
- The true memoir arc: 1963 marks the hinge from sheltered childhood to tested resilience—the first naming of loss as a companion to change.

Notable Quotes

- "Hope, in our house, wore work boots."
- "It's time to move on… I've had a good nine years, but it's time to do this on my own."
- "Freedom, I discovered, often came with borders—and consequences."
- "Holding on teaches the weight of love; letting go teaches its shape."
- "Every childhood has its bend in the road, the place where innocence blinks and begins to see."

Questions for reflection

- How does the chapter redefine "home" when loyalty pulls in multiple directions?
- Where do you see the line between discipline that forms character and discipline that silences curiosity?
- In what ways do community stories shape fear—and how can empathy revise those stories?
- What does Tippie's eastward pull reveal about inheritance and attachment across generations?
- How do faith and reality meet in the family's response to loss?

CHAPTER THREE
A River of Grief

But Jesus called for them, saying,
"Permit the children to come to Me, and do not hinder them, for the kingdom of God belongs to such as these."

LUKE 18:16

It was a bright Sunday in June 1963; the kind of afternoon that made the linoleum glow and the percolator hum seem like part of the sunshine. My maternal grandparents had come for one of their easy weekend visits. Farewells gathered slowly in our kitchen—Grandma Tuttle, as always, lingering with stories and one more thing; Grandpa patient in his quiet; Mom and Dad hovering near the table; Vincent and I orbiting the edges.

The phone rang.

Mom answered with her usual brightness. "Hello."

Her hand rose to her cheek, and in an instant, the room changed. The air thinned. We stood still, as if the kitchen itself were holding its breath. Mom's voice trembled; the color left her face.

"Oh no," she said, and the words fell like a stone.

Her head bowed into her free hand, the phone nearly slipping from her fingers. I stared, unable to ask the question already forming in my chest.

Fearing something terrible, I still wasn't prepared for what followed.

"Elmer's gone."

For a beat, the words made no sense. Gone? Where could he have gone?

"Oh, dear." Grandma Naomi's hand went to her mouth. Tears gathered. Grandpa sank into a chair, shaking his head as if to dislodge the news. My father stood motionless, a man braced against a wave he could not stop.

"Stevie, Elmer, and Allen were playing down by the river," Mom managed. "I'm not sure what happened, but Elmer drowned."

I didn't wait to hear the rest. The world had slipped sideways. I wanted to scream, but my voice would not come. There was only the ringing silence and the taste of fear at the back of my throat.

The Grain Bin

"Tag, you're it."

Elmer's fingertips grazed my shoulder, light but triumphant. He whooped, bouncing on his toes, all victory and grin. I spun, reaching for Vincent or one of my cousins, our feet clattering against the ribbed wire of the empty grain bin on Uncle Bernard's farm. Dust trembled in beams of light; our laughter echoed as if we were inside a giant bell.

Steve was Bernard and Cecelia Wilmes's oldest; Elmer came next. Allen and I were the same age. Bernard—my Uncle Bernard—was the eldest of George and Gertrude's family, and he and his wife, Cecelia, were my godparents. We pestered Mom and Dad for

Sunday drives to their farm, for the grandness of it, and for cousins who ran like the wind.

This was my only memory of Elmer alive. Try as I might, even in adulthood, nothing else would come when I reached for him—except one other image that waited decades before it surfaced: Elmer's stillness in a small casket.

My cousins began carrying a heavy cross that day, especially Steve. Neither he nor Elmer could swim. I often imagined Steve on the riverbank, frozen in terror, while Allen sprinted for help.

"It's a good thing Steve didn't try to save Elmer," my father said quietly. "They would have lost two sons."

Later, I sat on the cistern by the front porch of our house in rural Parnell and cried until I thought I would split apart. "No, God. Not Elmer. It can't be true." No one came to hush me. My parents let the grief take me—wise enough to know the wave had to spend itself. Death, unapologetic and heavy, had found our doorstep.

The River and the Aftermath

In the days that followed, we went to my cousins' home and said nothing because there was nothing to say. Rescue crews searched the riverbed. When they found him, hope drained from Aunt Cecelia as if a plug had been pulled. I watched her return to the house, led by Uncle Bernard—her body limp, a rag doll in a storm only she could feel.

This was not supposed to happen to our family, certainly not to my godparents. And yet it had. We stayed at my uncle's home for hours after the suddenness rearranged our lives.

"This is where it happened," Uncle Raymond said later, pointing to a scar of bank along the Nodaway River. The ground was rough, snagged with underbrush; the water slid past, indifferent and brown.

My uncles spoke in low voices, trying to piece together how it might have gone.

I was staring into the water when arms cinched around my waist, lifting me—flying me—over emptiness. For a heartbeat, I believed I would be dropped. Laughter erupted around me, and I realized it was my father's hands that held me fast. I tried to scream, but there wasn't enough air.

I laughed with them once my feet returned to earth, pretending the fear had not poured through me. That moment burrowed deep, a memory my mind hid away until it was ready. I know now my father was grieving too, sorting feelings the only way he knew—by turning dread into a joke and daring the river to answer back.

My cousins had only been playing. One moment, Elmer was here—the next, the river had taken him. Some part of me stayed on that bank, watching the current, learning how quickly a life can vanish and how long its echo remains.

The Wilmes boys were trained in stone: swallow your tears, square your shoulders, keep moving. My father carried that creed like a tool belt and tried to fit it on me. But I took after my mother—heart near the surface, champion of strays and underdogs, a boy who felt everything twice. Vincent mirrored Dad more closely, stepping into toughness as if it had always been his size.

As I grew, I kept bumping into the outline of the man my father wanted me to be. He passed down tradition like a baton; I held it and wondered whether I had to run the same race. Each time I pushed back—quietly, clumsily—I learned something about him, about me, and about the distance between our versions of strong.

Eternal rest

That summer I turned eight, the blur settled long enough for one clear scene: Price Funeral Home. Carpet that hushed your steps. Air so cool it raised gooseflesh—the sweet-heavy drift of flowers.

I walked with my parents to Elmer's casket, knelt, and looked at the stillness that used to be a boy. First family rosary of many—the beads clicked like small bones in someone's hands. I tried to pray. What came out was a thin thread of words that snapped as soon as I touched them. Emptiness spread in my chest, and the room seemed to tilt.

I followed my parents' lead to Bernard and Cecelia and the cousins—handshakes, nods, the choreography of grief. I'm sure I went to the funeral. Or maybe I didn't. Maybe my mother kept me back to spare me. Perhaps I was there, and my mind closed the door. Either way, I remember nothing of the burial—only the blank place where finality should be.

Some losses God tutors into us repeatedly. This was the first lesson. It would not be the last.

I took two memories and buried them deep: Elmer lying quietly in his casket, and my father's riverbank prank—the lift, the weightless moment, the laughter I borrowed to hide the fear. For years, I said my failure to learn to swim came from inheriting my mother's phobia. It never occurred to me that I was carrying my own.

Elmer's death had handed me a private terror. Drowning wasn't just a fear; it was a verdict whispered by water. In the end, I never learned to swim.

The Forbidden Topic

"I'm going to miss Elmer," I told Allen as we hovered near a doorway, catching the drift of adult voices inside my uncle's house.

"Yeah," he said, staring at nothing. "Sometimes it feels like a bad dream. I keep thinking he'll come downstairs and everything will be the same."

"How's Stevie?"

"Not good," he said. "He couldn't swim, you know."

"I know." And that was all I had.

We traded small stories, and our unsteady laughter slipped through the window. My mother saw us and excused herself from the murmurs inside. One look from her—urgent, pleading—and I knew what was coming.

"You boys need to go play," she said softly but firmly. "We don't have to talk about Elmer right now." She flicked her gaze toward Aunt Cecelia, then back to us. "Go on."

We ran because we didn't want to add any more pain to the day. I didn't know then that I'd take her instruction and carry it for years. After that afternoon, I hardly spoke Elmer's name. No one told me not to; no one told me to. Silence just felt easier—like tiptoeing through a room where someone is sleeping and never turning on the light.

Aftershocks and Small Joys

That winter, Bernard and Cecelia moved the family off the river bottom to a farm a few miles north of Maryville. We found ways to be children again: racing the ditches, playing "Mother May I" and "Red Light, Green Light," skidding in the pasture grass. Laughter loosened the tightness. We learned joy could coexist with absence, that play could make room for a ghost.

In the 1970s, visiting my grandmother's new house as a young man, my eyes always found the same thing: a black-and-white photo of Elmer, framed by exotic flowers and knick-knacks she tended like small altars. I never said, "Grandma, that's a beautiful picture. Tell me about him."

Instead, I wondered how she could keep it out where we could see it, yet not where it could see us. The photo comforted and unsettled me in equal measure, a reminder that he was gone, and that memory had its own stubborn life.

It never occurred to me that I could lift it from the shelf, hold it close, and let the grain-bin laughter come back. Those were treasures from before the river—meant to be remembered, not feared.

Jesus Calls the Child

I didn't understand it then, but that summer, my Catholic faith was the quiet net that kept me from falling all the way through. Only days after we buried Elmer, I started the two-week Catechism summer school—chalk dust in the air, box fans humming in the windows, a nun assisting the lay teachers, all moving like purposeful shadows across the linoleum.

At lunch, I opened my brown sack and found a single, perfect banana. It felt like a small treasure. I ate the rest quickly, then slipped out, heart thudding, and skittered through the rectory's back door toward the sanctuary. The church was empty—polished pews, the faint wax of extinguished candles, the sanctuary lamp a steady red eye.

I approached the altar, my hands shaking, and placed the banana in the exact center.

"I offer you this banana, God," I whispered.

I genuflected in a rush and fled, cheeks burning. If anyone had stopped me, I might have denied everything—like Peter, talking bravely until someone asked a question.

That afternoon, when the bell rang for recess, I darted back into the church. The air felt cooler, the quiet deeper. I stepped up to the altar and froze.

The banana was gone.

Something in me lifted—like a window cracking open on a stifling day. For an eight-year-old who had just lost his cousin, it felt monumental. I didn't tell a soul. Eventually, I forgot.

But God never forgets.

Circle of Life

Fall arrived with its familiar machinery. Dad mounted the orange corn picker on the nose of his Allis Chalmers D-17 and headed out, the wooden wagon bumping behind him. Trixie, tail wagging madly, trotted after, pretending the field belonged to all three of them. I went back to the hog shed with my shovel and my thoughts.

At supper, Dad came in quieter than usual. He lowered himself into the kitchen chair like a man sitting under a weight.

"I'm sorry," he said.

He stared at his hands. "Everything was going fine. I hollered at Trixie to get away from the picker. She did—for a while." His voice hitched. "Then there was this yelp and…"

I didn't wait for the rest. I already knew. Trixie was gone.

It became the start of a long procession of dogs I kept at arm's length. I told myself I still liked them, but I didn't have to love them. Love, I'd learned, had teeth—and loud machinery—and a way of disappearing when your back was turned.

Loss of Innocence

I couldn't have told you the name of the president on a typical morning at Parnell Elementary, but I remember the day I learned it by the sound of my classmate Bob Welch's voice outside the boys' bathroom.

"President Kennedy has been shot," he said.

That night, we gathered around the black-and-white TV—rabbit ears laced with tinfoil, news anchors in solemn suits. One more loss threaded itself through a year already frayed: Dad had decided we would move from my birth home; Tippie would be gone for good; the river had taken my cousin; the corn picker had taken Trixie. Now the country itself felt breakable.

The following Sunday, I lay on the floor in front of the TV, chin on my hands, when the picture turned electric. A man lunged. A crack like pop-fireworks split the air. Lee Harvey Oswald folded in real time, and I watched a second violence swallow the first. Dad bolted from his chair; I sprang up too, the shock moving through both of us like a current.

The nation's grief braided itself into my own—public mourning layered over private losses. I learned a boyhood version of endurance: add a little denial, keep moving, step into 1964 without looking back too hard.

But I had lost something else in 1963, something I couldn't name then: the certainty of my grandfather's strong hands around mine, the feeling that they could anchor me against anything.

Chapter reflections and takeaways

This chapter captures a poignant and heart-wrenching moment in the author's childhood, marked by the tragic drowning of his cousin Elmer. The narrative not only recounts the events surrounding this loss but also delves into the emotional aftermath, exploring themes of grief, memory, and the struggle between stoicism and vulnerability.

Key Themes

1. The Impact of Loss

- The suddenness of Elmer's death serves as a stark reminder of life's fragility.
- The author illustrates how loss reshapes family dynamics and individual identities.
- The scene transitions from joy and innocence to a profound sense of grief, highlighting how quickly life can change.

2. Grief and Silence

- The chapter portrays the complex nature of grief, particularly in a family setting.
- The author's mother encourages the children to avoid discussing Elmer, leading to a silence that permeates their lives. This reflects societal tendencies to sidestep discussions about death.
- The internal struggle of the author reveals how unprocessed grief can manifest, impacting personal relationships and emotional health.

3. Memory and Reflection

- The narrative intertwines memories of joyful moments with Elmer and the stark reality of his absence.
- The author grapples with remembering Elmer not just as a tragic figure but also as a source of joy and laughter.
- The black-and-white photograph of Elmer symbolizes the enduring presence of memory and the complexities of holding onto the past.

4. Stoicism vs. Emotional Expression

- The author contrasts the stoic approach of his father with his own more emotional nature.
- This dynamic illustrates the struggle between societal expectations of masculinity and the need for emotional expression.
- The chapter suggests that vulnerability can coexist with strength, challenging traditional notions of how grief should be handled.

Takeaways

- **Embrace Grief**: It's essential to acknowledge and express grief rather than suppress it. Open conversations about loss can foster healing.
- **Cherish Memories**: Memories, even painful ones, are valuable. They connect us to loved ones and remind us of the joy they brought to our lives.

- **Balance Strength and Vulnerability**: True strength lies in allowing oneself to feel and express emotions. Embracing vulnerability can lead to deeper connections with others.
- **The Complexity of Childhood**: Children process grief differently. Adults need to create safe spaces for children to explore their feelings and memories.
- **Coping Mechanisms**: Finding personal ways to cope with loss—whether through faith, humor, or creative expression—can provide comfort during difficult times.

This chapter serves as a powerful exploration of loss and its reverberations through time. It invites you to reflect on your own experiences of grief and the importance of making space for both sorrow and joy on life's journey. The narrative weaves together moments of happiness and heartache, creating a rich tapestry of human experience and ultimately reminding us of the enduring power of love and memory.

CHAPTER FOUR
Shattered Faith

"The Lord has called each of us; each is called by name. God is so great that he has time for each of us. He knows me, he knows each of us by name, personally. . .. I believe that we must meditate on this mystery again and again; God, the Lord, has called me, he calls me, he knows me and awaits my response as he awaited Mary's response, as he awaited the response of the Apostles."

ARCHBISHOP JOHN C. NEINSTEDT

Kyrie Eleison

(Lord, have mercy.)

I learned my first Latin by ear, bent over a phonograph in our farmhouse, mouthing syllables until they felt like mine. I was an eager altar boy in our little parish in Parnell, hungry to get it right. My timing was uncanny: I was coming of age just as the Second Vatican Council cracked open the Church's doors and let the English in.

Suddenly, the priest faced us. Altars were hauled out. Communion rails disappeared. Confessions in the dark gave way to face-to-face conversations. My father's generation didn't meet the changes with cheers. They tightened their jaws and waited it out, as if a storm might pass.

Before Vatican II, I walked beside the priest, paten in hand, gliding past a line of parishioners kneeling shoulder to shoulder at the rail.

I understood instinctively—because my parents had taught me—that laypeople did not touch the host, the Body and Blood of Christ.

And then, piece by piece, that certainty unspooled as Communion rails were removed, laypeople received the host in their hands—and then began to distribute it, nuns shed their black habits for street clothes, blending into the crowd.

In the convent east of Maryville, a stubborn remnant held the line—my father's aunt, Sister Genevieve, among them.

At home, the revolution set our table, whether we invited it or not. My parents tried to slow the current through Diocesan channels. To them, these were not mere customs but anchors. In time, I understood what they feared losing: reverence, mystery, the hush that makes room for God. Still, I was a child of the boom—made for adaptation, wary or not.

The Country Shifts Underfoot

Vietnam shadowed my childhood. Cities burned with racial tension. From our farm in northwest Missouri, it all felt distant—until it wasn't. Culture changes like weather: first a breeze, then a gale, and by the time it reaches you, you're already bracing.

I loved the Church. I trusted my parents. I didn't test a single boundary—until the day I did.

"Are Catholics the only ones who go to heaven?" I asked on the drive home from Mass. "What about other Christians? Don't they believe the same thing?"

My parents exchanged a glance.

"No one says people of other faiths don't go to heaven," my mother said gently.

My father added, "Jesus founded the Catholic Church. He told Peter, 'Upon this rock I will build my church.' Peter was the first pope. Other denominations came later."

"I see," I said. And I did—or almost. I stared out the window and wondered where the word Catholic appeared in the Bible. It was a small crack, but it let the questions in. I didn't know it then, but I belonged to a generation born to tug on the loose threads of certainty—faith and country both.

Beside me, my brother Vincent was silent, lost in his own world. He didn't spar with Dad the way I did. We were different in that way. I didn't yet know a more intimate upheaval was coming for me, with no catechism to prepare me for it.

God's Will Has A Say

No one told me God's will could rearrange your carefully stacked plans with a single touch. My mother's prayers were about to be answered, my life rerouted.

The day I came home from school, Mom sat Vincent and me at the kitchen table, her eyes bright.

"You know, boys," she said, "it's been just the four of us for a long time. But what would you think about a new arrival?"

She let the question hang, smiling. "I'm going to have a baby."

"Really?" Vincent burst into grins; his dimples flashed. I couldn't make sense of it. For so long, it had been just the two of us.

"Your new baby brother or sister should arrive around February," Mom said, glowing. "Lots of changes ahead."

"Yeah," I managed. "Wow. That's exciting."

I'm not sure I sounded convincing. I didn't compare notes with Vincent. I just walked out of our two-story farmhouse, down the gravel road, and toward the bridge. The news had landed like a fist in my gut.

I was eleven, in sixth grade, and ambushed by a fear I couldn't name. It felt like the day we moved to the farm in Parnell—like something cherished had been quietly taken. I stood over the creek and tossed stones, watching the ripples spread, thinking how late childhood and new babies didn't belong on the same list. Not mine, anyway.

The Stolen Goodbye

David arrived in February 1967. Dean followed in October of 1968, the year the world itself seemed to come apart. Dr. King was shot. Bobby Kennedy, too. I was thirteen, walking our green pastures and trying to make sense of death and God and the strange ache of hope.

In April, Uncle Jerry married Odelia Moffett, who stole my heart without trying. At twenty, she wore her brunette hair in a high beehive and carried herself with a modest grace that felt like a promise. Storybook or not, I believed in their wedding. They moved into my old boyhood home, and when we visited for supper, Odelia treated Vincent and me like visiting princes. It felt like stepping into a memory and finding it loved you back.

As eighth-grade graduation approached, Louise Stephenson came to our door with sorrow in tow. Her husband, Steve—top hat, pipe, laugh big enough to fill a room—had died of cancer. He and Dad were proud Knights of Columbus. I never got tired of

Steve's stories, their warmth still lingering in our living room long after he'd gone.

"Marvin and Vincent, I don't want you to go to his services," Louise said softly. "I want you to remember him the way he was."

I wanted to protest. Before I could, my mother put a hand on Louise's arm. "Don't worry," she said. "They'll keep the fond memories. That's a good idea."

Once again, I was protected from loss—as if grief were a draft to be kept out by shutting the door. When Louise drove away, Vincent and I went outside to play while my parents absorbed their own grief in quiet.

But the silence pressed on me. I needed to say goodbye. And this time, the goodbye was taken from me.

The Good Die Young

We packed into the Maryville Knights of Columbus Hall for a Christmas card party, the air sweet with cigar smoke and cinnamon. I played as Aunt Odelia's partner most of the night at the top table, her laughter tipping the cards in our favor as much as luck did. When we finally lost, she squeezed my shoulder and beamed. I didn't know I was collecting my last living memory of her.

On New Year's Eve, Mom and Dad went out to dance with Odelia and Uncle Jerry—music, sequins, the promise of a new year. Days later, a flu snapped into pneumonia, and death arrived with astonishing speed. No warning. No time to brace. My parents were stunned; I was unbelieving.

I prayed hard—for the first time with an adult's urgency—fervent, bargaining prayers borrowed from my catechism. Not long before, snowbound on a Sunday, I'd staged a family Mass in the living room, a blanket across my shoulders as makeshift vestments. I had believed then that God listened.

Uncle Jerry asked me to serve at the funeral. I carried the crucifix. At the back of the church, my hands gripped the wood while his grief rolled through the nave in raw, tearing sobs. I stared at the body on the cross and waited for meaning to land. Nothing came—only the hollowed-out hush of a sanctuary too quiet to bear.

Two days earlier, I'd walked in from chores to find my mother fall into my father's arms at the end of a phone call. "She's gone," she managed, and the words dissolved into tears. The kitchen—the same room where I'd heard "Elmer is dead" six years before—tilted under my feet. We had just laughed and played cards at Christmas. How could the world change its mind that fast?

I fled upstairs, threw myself onto the bed, and clawed at heaven with the only question that mattered: "Why, God? Why take someone so young?"

There was no answer, only a silence that hardened in me like winter ice. Standing before Odelia's casket, still clutching the crucifix, I watched Uncle Jerry choke on the questions I couldn't swallow. Something foundational cracked. I kept the outward shape of faith—the responses, the folded hands—but inside I packed God away like a toy I'd outgrown. Later, after I left home, I'd drift from church while insisting I still believed.

The reason felt simple to thirteen-year-old me: I asked, and God said nothing. I pleaded, and she died. Pneumonia joined water on my private list of unreasonable fears. With Odelia's passing, a bright, gentle part of me went with her.

High School Angst

February 1970 brought Norbert Lee and a small boom in our household economy. My parents turned the basement into a family room for five boys—Vincent, David, Dean, Norbert, and me. They moved their bedroom to the front room, added a bathroom and a utility room, and hired a parish carpenter who smelled of cut pine and coffee. I tagged along on shopping trips for carpet and ceiling tiles, the grown-up thrill of choosing a pattern as intoxicating as the thrill of driving would someday be. The house hummed with saws and hope.

With more little brothers came more responsibility. I became the default babysitter—bottles, diapers, lullabies, and the tired that sits behind your eyes. Still, I never doubted I was loved. Dad and I fought like summer storms—brief and loud. Mom was the barometer, keeping the weather from breaking the windows.

Somewhere between mowing and feeding calves, a writer woke up in me. I told stories in my head as I pushed the mower, in long, green stripes. I knew I wouldn't be a farmer. College shimmered in the distance like a lake, and I was thirsty.

As a freshman, I went on a discernment retreat to Conception Abbey. Grandpa Wilmes wanted a priest in the family—someone to follow his sister's vocation—and I tried to want it, too. But the bells, the hours of prayer, the quiet—it didn't open for me. Maybe it was my unsettled faith after Odelia. Perhaps it was the stage lights I couldn't stop imagining. Either way, the call didn't come. God's ways, I was learning, are not our ways—at least not the tidy kind.

In the fall of my junior year, while I was playing the lead in our class play—feeding a creative hunger the fields couldn't satisfy—Linda Michelle was born. In March of 1973, the spring I graduated, we welcomed Nancy Charlene. Our family continued to grow as my world lifted its anchors.

By then, the horizon had shifted. The house was fuller, the nights were louder, the questions deeper. I stood in a borrowed cap and gown, the Missouri wind at my back, and felt it: a brave new world, waiting.

Reflections and takeaways

- A coming-of-age memoir set against the seismic shifts of Vatican II, the turbulence of the 1960s, and the intimate upheavals within a Missouri farm family.
- The narrator moves from reverent certainty to questioning faith, catalyzed by personal loss (Odelia's death), cultural revolutions, and expanding family responsibilities.
- The chapter closes with the stirrings of vocation (not to priesthood but to storytelling), and a widening horizon at graduation.

Core themes and motifs

- Reverence vs. reform: Old liturgical certainties "unspool" as rails come down and Latin gives way to English. The chapter captures both the beauty of reverence and the ache of change. Cultural and church transitions occur gradually, much like changing weather—shifting from a gentle breeze to a strong gale—in both global events (such as Vietnam or civil rights) and personal life (such as new siblings or moving rooms).
- The education of grief: Being shielded from funerals creates a "stolen goodbye," culminating in an intimate confrontation with loss at Odelia's funeral.
- The silence of God: After fervent prayer goes unanswered, faith's outward form remains while the inner trust fractures—"a silence that hardened in me like winter ice."

- Vocation and identity: A discernment retreat reveals a "holy no," while the mower's green stripes become lines of narrative—a writer awakening.
- Memory as place: Homes, bridges, kitchens, and sanctuaries become charged spaces where identity is formed and re-formed.

Spiritual reflections

- "Kyrie eleison" as refrain: Mercy stands at the threshold of change, grief, and identity. The chapter's heart-prayer remains simple when certainty dissolves.
- The cost of shielding children from death: Well-meant protection can stall grief and deepen spiritual disorientation.
- When vocation says "no": A true calling often emerges by subtraction; rejecting the wrong path makes space for the right one.
- Reverence reclaimed: The fear of losing "hush" and "mystery" points to a more profound need—to protect spaces where God can be heard, even in silence.

Key takeaways

- Honor both reverence and reform: Change is inevitable; safeguarding mystery is a choice.
- Let children face grief with guidance, not isolation; goodbyes are formative.
- Faith can mature through honest lament; silence is not absence, but it wounds when community can't name it.

- Vocation can be discovered in the ordinary (mowing lawns, basement remodels) as much as in monasteries.
- Cultural upheaval externalizes inner storms—naming one helps weather the other.
- Family expansion is both a blessing and an identity crisis; love includes making room for ambivalence.
- Rituals matter—because they hold us when belief feels thin.

Memorable images and lines (briefly noted)

- Paten and rail: The boy gliding beside the priest—embodied reverence.
- "Certainty unspooled": The concrete becoming thread—lucid metaphor for reform.
- "Silence hardened like winter ice": A felt definition of spiritual desolation.
- The crucifix borne during Odelia's funeral: Faith's symbol heavy with unanswered anguish.
- The mower's green stripes: A writer tracing his first lines on a living page.

Questions to sit with

- How do we hold reverence without resisting necessary renewal?
- What losses did shielding from grief prevent—and what wounds did it cause?
- Where does mercy appear when God feels silent?

- What small, repetitive tasks in our lives are quietly teaching us our vocation?

Personal invitation / Application

- Practice a weekly "hush"—five minutes of intentional silence—to reintroduce reverence in a noisy era.
- Write one paragraph about a "stolen goodbye" or a goodbye you were allowed to have—and what it changed in you.
- Name one ordinary task that might also be your apprenticeship in a vocation.

Kyrie eleison—Lord, have mercy on our changing, grieving, and becoming.

CHAPTER FIVE

Material Things

"Never forget what's important in life. Material things can be replaced, but important people can't."

SONYA PARKER

My business teacher preached a simple gospel: "Become an accountant, and you will have the world by the tail." I grabbed that tail with both hands. Numbers promised order, respectability, a clean-lined future. So, I headed off to college with ledgers on my mind and certainty in my pocket.

First-semester economics blew a hole in that tidy ship. I went down fast, surprised by how quickly a life of columns and balance sheets could sink me. I didn't yet know that numbers ran crosswise to the undiscovered rhythm in me—the creative beat that wouldn't announce itself until much later, when I started writing letters home in the service and felt the quiet power of sentences carrying more truth than I could say out loud.

Even before that, the signs were there. Pushing the mower in tight loops across our yard, I'd catch my mother watching me through the kitchen window while my mouth ran a mile a minute. I was narrating my own epics—plotting danger in the ditches, rescuing heroes by the fence post. I told stories while rounding up cattle, while walking the beans, while walking anywhere at all. No one at my small high school spotted it. No one encouraged it.

"To even think for one moment that a Wilmes could be a creative soul?"

I didn't, not really. I played it safely. I landed the lead in our junior play—Margie and the Wolfman—and we wrung a single night of applause from weeks of practice. I loved every second of it, but I still didn't name it as a strength. I didn't trust my own gifts.

Two forces tugged at my future then: my father and Grandma Naomi. She was a schoolteacher and saw herself in me, sometimes too much. She'd read the room and take my side over Vincent's in a pecking order I never noticed, but the message was clear: you're firstborn; bear the load. Dad thought I should work a year before college, get some grit under my nails. Grandma wouldn't hear of it. I'd ranked fourth in my class. In my mind, college wasn't a question; it was a destination.

Mom let me decide on my own.

So that fall, I enrolled at Northwest Missouri State University. No campus tours, no big decision tree—Grandma had studied there, it was close, and I could commute. I told myself I knew what I was doing. I didn't. The need to earn money cornered me fast, and I made the kind of choice you make when you don't know yourself: I tried to muscle through everything at once. By the summer of 1974, I was in a small Maryville apartment, working at Regal Textile—a diaper factory—breathing lint and fluorescent hum, muscles sore by midnight.

By the fall of my sophomore year, I had abandoned accounting for computer science, as if I could outrun the truth with a new major. It didn't help. My grades slid, and I kept the slide quiet, especially from Grandma. I was losing the thread and couldn't say it out loud.

Maybe that's why the maroon 1974 Formula Firebird looked like salvation on four wheels. My current car—a 1967 Ford Galaxie 500 — was Dad's compromise, purchased with a practical mindset and an eye toward passing it to my brother when I was done. It had enough power to keep a high school senior honest, but the Firebird glittered like forbidden fruit—price tag: $4,200. With Dad's signature, it could be mine.

I drove home for the meeting with the salesman and my father. The Firebird sat in our driveway like a promise. I saw the back of the salesman's head and felt, for once, that I had an ally inside our walls. Dad puffed his pipe and weighed things the way he always did—with that middle-of-the-road philosophy I knew so well. I kept my mouth shut. Sometimes the smartest argument is silence. He finally nodded, and with that, I inherited more than a car. I inherited responsibility.

The Firebird delivered—too well. Overnight, I was popular. The guys dared me to race down the Ravenwood bottom. I obliged. It changed me, or I let it.

Then came the fall of 1974. The recession bit down hard. At the factory, we learned our fates from a note taped to the door: four days this week, then three, then two. My paychecks thinned, my car payments didn't. One Saturday night I added stupidity to scarcity—showing off, too fast on gravel, and the Firebird punished me for it. Meanwhile, my GPA sank for the third straight semester, stubbornly below a 2.0.

The mask slipped. The story I'd been telling—of the kid with the plan, the job, the car, the future—stopped holding. I needed an intervention. Or maybe I needed what I'd needed all along: a miracle, yes—but also the courage to call my life by its true name and start again.

By the fall of 1974, my life had narrowed to a dim hallway: nights at the factory, mornings I should've been in class, afternoons too tired to tell the truth. I had already wrapped my Firebird around a pole and still believed I could burn the candle at both ends and outrun the smoke. The paychecks shrank. The factory slowed. My sixty-dollar apartment wore the scent of stale coffee and denial. I told my parents I was fine. I wasn't. I was sinking, and I didn't yet have the word for it.

I kept the charade going—pretending I went to class after the 8 a.m. shift, pretending I could keep up, pretending failing at school wasn't already a foregone conclusion. You cannot serve two masters, but I stubbornly tried: good son, good worker, weekend cowboy charging down gravel roads, gunning the Firebird at country drag races. I was trying to please my dad, my grandmother, and a version of myself I couldn't stand to look at in the mirror.

One afternoon, I left the television on and fell asleep. When I woke, Fess Parker was striding through the wilderness donning a coon skin cap as Daniel Boone, sure-footed and sure of himself in a way I hadn't felt in years. It was a ridiculous catalyst, but something inside me shifted. I shut off the TV, grabbed my keys, and drove to Parnell to see my best friend, Dan Welch.

When I locked my apartment door behind me, a still, small voice rose like a pulse in my chest: 'Things are about to change for the better.' I couldn't have told you why I believed it, only that I did.

Something about that night felt marked, as if a corner of my life had been dog-eared by a hand I couldn't see.

Dan's parents' basement smelled like pool chalk dust and teenage years. He skipped racking the pool balls, slapped me hard on the back, and grinned like he had a secret.

"I've been talking to a recruiter," he said. "Buddy plan. We can join the Marine Corps, and I can be a PFC right out of the gate."

I told him he was insane. Dan had pitched harebrained schemes before; this one was a new altitude. His brother wandered in, took the measure of me, and bet me fifty dollars I'd never do it. That stung. Dan kept talking. He had a way of doing that—pressing a finger on the bruise until you admitted where the pain was coming from. I left that night convinced he was still crazy, and as usual, I would ignore him and keep stumbling forward.

The recruiter found me anyway. I was at my parents' house when the phone rang. My mother—who had worn her knees out praying for me long before I learned how to pray for myself—said I should at least hear the man out. Fine, I thought. I'll give him thirty minutes and then show him the door. I'd already been suspended for a semester. No one had written "depression" on a chart, but I was swimming deep in it.

I went in ready to say no. Instead, in that half hour, the man tossed me a line I didn't know I was desperate to catch. I signed papers committing to four years in the United States Marine Corps. Impulsive? Absolutely. Nothing was binding until I passed the physical in Kansas City, but a line had been crossed. The rearview went cloudy.

There's a streak in the Wilmes men—call it German stubbornness or simply the way a decision feels once it locks into place.

When we step over a line, we don't step back. I couldn't explain it to anyone. My life was a shambles anyway: the factory had slowed, the car payment was a weight around my neck, I'd flunked college. This felt like a chance to start over.

Did I know what I wanted to do with my life? No. More urgently: did I know who I was? Also no.

I knew, however, who the still, small voice belonged to. It was God, knocking. I was no saint. I wasn't the clean-cut senior who once imagined himself an accountant in a crisp tie, making big money. Throughout high school, I'd daydreamed wildly—Navy blue uniforms, a priest's collar, a painting truck with my name on the door, a quiet desk where I wrote stories after a long day because books had taught me to love words. In the end, I had been living out other people's plans, not my own. God was stirring the nest, making the familiar prickly and uncomfortable until escape felt like the only way to save myself. My creative gifts simmered beneath the surface, but I'd tried to bury them under a glossy American Dream: a car I could barely afford and a mask that didn't fit. As 1974 collapsed into winter, the mask slipped. The truth had teeth.

I told my parents what I'd done. My father stood at the bottom of the stairs, the way he had once before in 1962 when he announced he was moving on. I knew that stance—jaw set, eyes steady, the whole house holding its breath.

"Four years," he said finally. "That's a long time."

He had done two years in the Marine Corps himself. Two had been long enough. He had earned the right to be uneasy for his eldest son. There would be no backing out once I passed that physical.

Two years earlier, I had jumped for joy, tossing a fence post into the back of a wagon when the radio announced President Nixon had ended the draft. I had escaped Vietnam, war, the uniform, the weight of duty. So why was I now on a bus to Kansas City while Dan stayed back on the farm, tending chores? It had been his idea—and there I was, rolling toward commitment while he remained in the life I thought I wanted.

At the processing station, everything was fluorescent and loud. Forms slid across counters. Pens ran out of ink and were replaced by pens that didn't. I signed where they told me to sign. The bus ride back was a blur of highway lights and the rattling certainty that I had boarded something larger than a vehicle.

Basic training made it official. The first night, the air tasted like metal and adrenaline. I lay on a thin mattress surrounded by strangers and certainty and realized I might have made the biggest mistake of my life. The shouting, the cadence, the stripping away, it felt like Hell had a postal address. But when I listened beneath the noise, the same quiet voice I'd heard at my apartment door was there, steady as a heartbeat.

You cannot serve two masters.

I had tried. Work and school. The Firebird and the future. My father's hopes, my grandmother's prayers, and a young man's hunger to outrun himself. That night, in the pits of basic training, sweating under a blanket that didn't quite reach my feet, I understood I hadn't come to the Marines to learn how to fight. I had come to learn how to surrender—first to orders, eventually to purpose.

I didn't yet know what I wanted to be. But I was beginning to discover who I was. And Who was calling. It was the first time He spoke to me that clearly. It wouldn't be the last.

Reflections and Takeaways

A young man pursues a respectable path (accounting/computers) while suppressing a creative core.

Status and speed (the Firebird) become a mask during a season of economic scarcity and personal collapse.

A surprising invitation (the Marines) catalyzes surrender, identity, and faith—moving from control to calling.

Core Themes

- Identity vs. Expectation: The tension between family scripts (Dad, Grandma Naomi), small-town norms, and the narrator's buried creative self.
- Control vs. Surrender: From muscling through jobs and classes to accepting discipline and purpose.
- Illusion vs. Truth: "The mask slipped." The Firebird, GPA, and popularity hide a deepening depression and dislocation.
- Providence and Choice: The still, small voice—subtle yet decisive—meeting human agency at a breaking point.
- Masculinity Reframed: Popularity, daredevil bravado, and stoicism give way to humility, obedience, and spiritual attentiveness.

Seasons Change

- The Setup: "Numbers promised order" self-chosen for stability and approval.
- The Unraveling: Factory nights, dwindling shifts, wrecked car, sliding grades, more profound isolation.

- The Pivot: A trivial TV moment (Daniel Boone) cracks the inertia; friend Dan's recruiter pitch becomes a lifeline.
- The Commitment: Signing with the Marines reframes the crisis as a start-over.
- The Revelation: Basic training strips pretense; the lesson isn't combat—it's surrender and purpose.

Spiritual Reflections

- Calling often comes as a whisper, not a trumpet.
- Grace arrives through unlikely messengers: a TV rerun, a recruiter, a friend's taunt.
- Surrender isn't passivity; it's aligned agency—obeying a purpose bigger than ego or expectation.
- "You cannot serve two masters" becomes both moral and vocational clarity.

Things you cannot control

- The 1974 recession sharpens the stakes—fewer shifts, thinner paychecks, shrinking options.
- Rural midwestern culture: duty, family hierarchy, respectability; little space for naming creative gifts.
- Intergenerational echoes: Father's Marine service complicates approval and fear; Grandma's academic pride fuels pressure.

Memorable Lines

- "Numbers promised order, respectability, a clean-lined future."
- "The Firebird sat in our driveway like a promise."
- "The mask slipped."
- "The truth had teeth."
- "I had come to learn how to surrender—first to orders, eventually to purpose."

Personal Takeaways for Readers

- Pay attention to early sparks: the yard "epics" foretold the writer long before the transcripts did.
- Beware the glow of symbols (cars, titles) that promise identity but deliver debt and drift.
- When life narrows to a "dim hallway," small obediences can open the door.
- The right structure (discipline, community, mission) can rescue gifts that chaos buries.
- Sometimes you don't find your career first—you find your character.

Questions for Reflection

- Where am I serving two masters right now?
- What early loves (often dismissed) keep resurfacing?
- Which "Firebirds" in my life are really masks?

- What structure or community could help me surrender toward purpose?
- Where might a still, small voice be speaking beneath the noise?

Practical Applications

- Inventory your desires: make two lists—what you're good at vs. what gives you life; notice overlaps and gaps.
- Name your masks: one status symbol or story you're propping up; decide one concrete step to release it.
- Build in surrender: adopt a practice (e.g., daily silence, mentorship, service) that cultivates attention and humility.
- Seek structure: if you're spiraling, choose a disciplined environment (course, program, service, apprenticeship) that realigns you.
- Tell the truth early: ask one trusted person to reality-check your current "narrative."

Final Takeaway

This chapter is a compelling testament to how collapse can be a compass. The narrator doesn't discover a profession as much as he discovers a posture—surrendered, listening, and finally aligned with a truer self. The rest of the story can grow from there.

CHAPTER SIX
Call to Conversion

"Now there was a man of the Pharisees named Nicodemus, a ruler of the Jews. This man came to Jesus by night and said to him, 'Rabbi, we know that you are a teacher come from God, for no one can do these signs that you do unless God is with him.' Jesus answered him, 'Truly, truly, I say to you, unless one is born again, he cannot see the kingdom of God.' Nicodemus said to him, 'How can a man be born when he is old? Can he enter a second time into his mother's womb and be born?' Jesus answered, 'Truly, truly, I say to you, unless one is born of water and the Spirit, he cannot enter the kingdom of God.' That which is born of the flesh is flesh, and that which is born of the Spirit is spirit. Do not marvel that I said to you, 'You must be born again.' The wind blows where it wishes, and you hear its sound, but you do not know where it comes from or where it goes. So, it is with everyone who is born of the Spirit."

John 3: 3-8

The Ultimate Denial

June 1975, Phase Two, Camp Pendleton.

I was on maintenance duty when a runner found me in the field and sent me to the main office. The fluorescent hallway hummed like a beehive.

I snapped to attention. "PFC Wilmes reporting, sir."

"At ease, Marine." The drill instructor's voice shifted, flint to felt. "I have bad news, Wilmes. Your cousin Steven was killed in a car accident. My condolences to you and your family."

The words hit and slid off like rain on wax. "What?"

"You can call home. If you need to go back for the funeral, we'll make it happen. I can't guarantee you'll rejoin this platoon, but you can pick up where you left off."

Steve—Aunt Dee's eldest of our next generation—had grown up inside the same tight fences I had, his parents wrapping him in an extra layer of protection after 1963, after Elmer drowned. Now twenty-three, he left behind a wife, a three-year-old son, and an infant daughter. Another son is gone. Another hole in a family that had already learned how grief rearranges the furniture.

Boot camp had stripped me to muscle memory. Home felt like a foreign country. And I knew one thing with cold certainty: if I stepped out, it would be hard to step back in. My platoon was my family now. I wanted to finish with them.

"Sir, I'll be all right if I don't go home. I want to graduate as soon as possible."

The DI studied me, something like respect flaring, then dimming. "You sure?"

"Yes, sir."

"Call your folks. Get the details. Dismissed."

As a Marine, I chose mission. As a cousin who had grown up alongside Steve, I chose not to walk through the valley with the people who needed me. Denial wore the same uniform I did.

With Steve's death, I became the oldest living cousin in the George Wilmes line. My godparents—his parents—were laying a second son to rest in twelve years. When I finally came home on leave between boot camp and Millington, Tennessee, I met my brother Roland for the first time—he'd waited to be born until I'd marched across the grinder. I hugged him, then dodged the silence. I had not gone to the funeral. I didn't call my godparents. I didn't find Allen, Steve's brother, and said the only words that ever matter I'm here.

Instead, Steve's death became a statistic I discussed with my parents on the drive from the airport. In the vacuum of recruit training, feeling had been punished out of me. Later, sitting with Allen, I watched the quiet settle heavily between us. I matched his silence with my own, mistaking reflection for comfort because I had no language for grief.

Steve had carried 1963 like a stone in his pocket—the day he saw his brother drown. I knew that much. What I didn't know yet was how much we shared: the weight born by firstborn sons, the way responsibility can feel like a cross you don't get to set down. In 1975, I traded the role of older brother and babysitter for a uniform and orders. He carried the burden of a brother's death; mine would become the burden of my family's needs. At home, we didn't talk about Elmer. Now, I haven't talked about Steve. Silence had become second nature.

My first postings mapped a new life: San Diego, Memphis, El Toro, and Beaufort. I was twenty, a Missouri farm kid stepping into the bright, loud real world. I embraced the adventure, but the ache traveled with me.

Lifeline from the Past

Summer of 1976, Beaufort, South Carolina. My friend and co-worker Jerry pitched a run to Disney World. We'd swing through Zephyrhills, Florida, to leave his motorcycle with his aunt. He'd ride the bike. I'd drive my Firebird. I made one thing clear: I wasn't getting on that motorcycle.

We stopped for dinner in Georgia. Jerry rubbed his eyes. "I'm wiped. Can you take the bike?"

My friends had a way of asking for the impossible. I said yes.

Helmet on, wind in my face, dread in my gut. The interstate blurred. At the next exit, I tried to ease into the curve and felt it immediately. I was coming in too hot, too fast. Panic flared. I grabbed at control and lost more of it.

Jesus, save me!

The prayer arrived before my mind formed the words, a catechism echo from second grade. A gust hit the bike sideways. The world tilted. I flew. Headfirst. Asphalt. A sound like a drum inside my skull. Then sliding, and the strangest, sharpest thought: I'm alive.

I lifted my head in time to see the Firebird disappear around the bend. Jerry hadn't seen me go down. The bike lay broken and, later, hung from a tow truck like a scold. A stranger knelt beside me. "You all right?"

I stood on shaking legs, caught between dread—Jerry's face when he saw his bike—and wonder that my heart was still beating. The police came. Jerry doubled back. He saw the motorcycle before he saw me.

I refused medical treatment—stubborn, poor choice—and paid for it the next day when every bone staged a protest. We reached his aunt's, who answered the door with the universal look of family surprise: you could have called. The following day we ferried across to the Magic Kingdom, the water black and glassy, my body aching, my spirit strangely alert.

I believed God had answered that roadside prayer, the one a teacher planted in me years earlier. That belief cracked something open. It didn't promise a rose garden—initially, Jesus never does; usually, it's a rock-bottom moment—but it offered life, and more of it.

Back in Beaufort, I started to search. I picked up Hal Lindsey's *The Late Great Planet Earth* and read it between Mess Duty shifts, the barracks quiet when my roommate worked nights. Jesus, the one who died for me, walked off the page and into the room. A new understanding settled in: Father, Son, Spirit—separate and one. I had felt the Spirit before and didn't know it: the gust that pushed the motorcycle sideways while my life flickered past like slides I didn't always like.

I had all but stopped going to church. In boot camp, I attended one Sunday Mass and then chose my free time to write letters home to Mom. Those weekly letters kept me plugged into the Missouri farm, but not into God. In Beaufort, I felt far from Him—and closer than I realized.

I devoured the book until the weight of it pressed on me. Perfection wasn't possible. The more I read, the more my guilt rose—the old knots tightening into something honest. One night, the conviction of my sins hit so hard I hurled the book at the wall. Then I sat in the quiet, breathing hard, waiting for a voice I'd heard before, small and steady.

Mercy In The Margins

I picked the book back up and kept reading. The pages didn't feel heavy anymore; my chest did.

Jesus emerged in a new light—less judge, more rescuer. The angry God of my youth receded into a God still just, but now unmistakably merciful. Hope slipped into the room and sat down beside me.

The Night Everything Broke Open

Summer, 1976. Beaufort barracks. A thin mattress, a humming fan, the quiet of an empty room. I surrendered. No speeches. No witnesses. Just yes.

I was slain in the Spirit—hit not by lightning, but by mercy. Tears came hard and clean. A current ran through me from crown to soles. I felt Jesus move through my body like power and gentleness braided together. I will never forget it.

That night a relationship began that still holds. It's been tested by life, by my own stubbornness, and by the knots of my Catholic upbringing—but the line never snapped. I wandered, but He didn't.

I wasn't suddenly perfect, far from it. I drifted; He tugged me back. That new allegiance also lit a fuse between my father and me—our arguments about religion got louder—but underneath the noise, a simple truth stayed put: Jesus had my hand, even when I tried to pull away.

The book was merely a doorway. Years later, the path would loop me back into a deeper return to the Catholic Church I never truly left.

Catholic Roots, Born-Again Fire

I've always been Catholic—cradle, cultural, conflicted.

My born-again encounter didn't erase that; it supplemented it.

For years, I struggled to practice consistently, like many do. Still, being Catholic quietly steered my choices.

My faith shifted from head-knowledge to heart-fire. I devoured spiritual books for a decade, but even on paper forms I checked "Catholic" while still questioning parts of what I said I believed.

God met me where I was. In time, He nudged me toward where I needed to be.

Signs I Could Finally Read

God reassured me about Odelia and Elmer: they were home. The Christ I carried at Odelia's funeral wasn't fixed on the cross—He had risen. I'd known that in my head; as a kid, Easter meant ending the fast and demolishing a basket of candy. I never bought the Easter Bunny; Santa was easier. But now resurrection moved from doctrine to oxygen.

Baptized in water as an infant.

Confirmed at ten.

Baptized in the Holy Spirit at twenty-one.

Three mile-markers on the same road.

Do I believe God has a plan for each of us? Yes. I was learning to stop leaning on my own understanding. Proverbs had come alive.

A Writer Begins To Wake

My letters home had been more than updates; they were early journals. After my conversion, a new hunger surfaced. I started dreaming of writing in earnest and began my first piece, aptly titled The Jungle.

God calls His children by many paths. In 1976, He called me home—and handed me tools for the work ahead. He also made me face a lifetime of denial I'd been perfecting. My mother never heard the full story of the motorcycle crash, and that's a mercy I won't undo. But I became a loud advocate for helmets; I'm convinced mine saved my life that day.

How does God prepare a writer to persevere and tell the truth? He puts him through the paces. I didn't know it then, but my first twenty-one years were only the prologue. The lessons were just beginning. And this time, I was finally awake to learn them.

Reflections and Takeaways

This chapter traces a raw inner journey from denial to surrender—moving through military discipline, family grief, a brush with death, and a surprising encounter with mercy. It's a testimony of how silence can calcify into habit, and how grace breaks it open—quietly, insistently, and personally.

Brief Summary

- In Marine boot camp, the narrator learns of Cousin Steve's death and chooses duty over attending the funeral—another layer of family silence around grief.
- A near-fatal motorcycle accident becomes a turning point: a spontaneous prayer ("Jesus, save me!") and a spared life awaken spiritual hunger.
- Reading *The Late Great Planet Earth* intensifies conviction and catalyzes a profound experience of the Holy Spirit—"Slain in the Spirit."
- The narrator embraces a born-again relationship with Jesus while remaining rooted in Catholic identity—an integration rather than a departure.
- Imperfection persists (family tensions, inconsistency), but a sustaining thread emerges: "not perfect, held."

Core Themes

- Duty vs. grief: Choosing the mission over mourning reveals the cost of emotional suppression.
- The legacy of loss: Family trauma (Elmer's drowning) shapes how pain is carried—"grief rearranges the furniture."

- Denial as uniform: "Denial wore the same uniform I did" captures how identity and avoidance can merge.
- Grace interrupts: A roadside plea turns into a life reoriented—not by fear, but by mercy.
- Faith as integration: Catholic sacraments meet charismatic experience—head-knowledge transitions into heart-fire.
- Imperfect discipleship: Growth is cyclical—drifting, tugging back, held by a faithful God.

Narrative Arc & Turning Points

- Notification of Steve's death → decision not to go home → deepening silence.
- Motorcycle crash → instinctive prayer → survival → spiritual search.
- Reading → conviction and resistance (throwing the book) → surrender → charismatic encounter.
- Ongoing journey → tensions with father, recommitment, and a seed of vocation as a writer.

Key Takeaways

- Saying "no" to grief is a choice with relational costs—silence is not comfort.
- Crisis can surface childhood faith unexpectedly, becoming a lifeline.
- Conviction and mercy often arrive together; one without the other can distort faith.

- Spiritual experiences don't require abandoning one's roots; integration is possible and fruitful.
- Being "held" is more transformative than being "perfect."
- Identity as firstborn can shape burdens—and also awaken a call to responsibility rightly ordered.
- Faith journeys often retrace earlier steps: baptism → confirmation → Spirit-filled renewal.
- Writing emerges as a response to grace—an act of witness and meaning-making.

Personal Reflection Questions

- Where have I chosen "mission" over presence with grieving people—and what did that cost?
- What prayers rise instinctively in crisis? What do they reveal about my deepest trust?
- Where has conviction felt heavy—and how might mercy share the weight?
- How can I honor my spiritual roots while remaining open to fresh encounters with God?
- What silence in my life masquerades as strength?

Practices to Live This Out

- Reach out where silence once ruled: make the call, write the note, show up.
- Name and ritualize losses—funerals, memorials, or private acts of remembrance.
- Pair reading with prayer: let doctrine become dialogue.

- Hold tension with family graciously—argue less to win, more to understand.
- Journal your own "lifeline" moments; track grace as it threads through your story.

Final Takeaway

This chapter is a witness to the God who meets us on asphalt and in barracks, in old books and new tears—guiding us from denial to presence, from fear to mercy, from silence to voice.

PART TWO

CRISIS OF FAITH

I can't change the direction of the wind, but I can adjust my sails to always reach my destination.

Jimmy Dean

CHAPTER SEVEN
Earthquake

"Denial is the shock absorber for the soul.
It protects us until we are equipped to cope with reality."

C.S. Lewis

Hobbs, New Mexico, 1983.

I pressed my knees to the space heater in my two-room cottage and let it burn a seam of warmth into my shins. Outside, the winter set records—snow stacked against the door, wind strafing the eaves, a sky the color of tin. Inside, the phone sat like a lifeline. At the station, a few of the guys had hedged their bets—stocks, oil leases, black gold. Radio was their side project, a toy they tinkered with between dividends. I had only the toy.

After four years in the United States Marine Corps, I came home changed—quieter, steadier, carrying a faith I hadn't found in my own backyard. I enrolled in college, chased microphones and deadlines, and told myself I was building something. When the job market went dry, I took the offer in the New Mexico desert and called it a starter block. The truth was more straightforward: I was scraping by. Each payday meant math on napkins and late calls home to hear a voice that meant I had somewhere to go back to.

I chose the creative road because it felt like a calling. So far, the road had only offered more conviction than cash. And then there was Regina.

Love's sting

Missouri, January 1980, three years prior.

The wipers beat time across a windshield furred with snow, and my heart kept pace. I'd been out of the service a year and had begun to believe again in improbable things—Jesus's words about telling mountains to move.

I picked the wrong mountain, but it moved anyway.

Months earlier, my final deployment took me to Japan, and somewhere in the middle, the schedule threw in a three-week detour to the Philippines. Jim—my best friend—and I fought the idea, then went anyway. We'd just spent three careless days in Maui, and my spirit still felt like it could ride a thermal.

One night on base in Subic Bay, we ducked into the club. That's where I saw her. Taller than most, slender, a kind of quiet light about her. Our eyes caught across the room and held.

"Hi, my name is Regina," she said, drifting to our table as if on a slipstream. "Can I get you something?"

"Rum and Coke," I managed, nearly mute with wonder.

Hours unspooled. Families, hopes, fears. We were both from big broods. She was the oldest of eight, looking after her father. We laughed until the club's noise became a backdrop, and a connection I couldn't name took shape between us.

Then the clock started to matter. With my time so short, Regina eased back—short answers, early goodbyes, a smile that didn't linger.

I had no defenses for that, only questions. When the C-130 clawed into the sky toward Japan, it carried my body and left the rest.

Back in Hawaii, then Missouri, I tried to file the whole thing under "what if." I dated a girl in my hometown, went to work, and went to church. But Regina's face kept surfacing—on a TV screen in a dark living room, in a car window at a red light.

I did the unthinkable: I called her. She answered, stunned. Letters followed through the summer of '79, the ink a bridge neither of us trusted, and both of us crossed. In one of them, I asked her to marry me. She said yes.

And so here I was, steering through a whiteout toward the airport, breath fogging the cab, mind sprinting ahead to our first moment on American ground together. I pictured a kiss, a laugh, the quick warmth of everything we'd promised on paper.

When she stepped off the plane, her face held the same bright radiance I remembered. I moved in to hug her. She lifted her ticket and tapped it lightly against my head.

"Hi," she said.

I stood there, dumbfounded, and reached for her bag. On the drive through hills buried in snow, the silence between us felt as cold as the air seeping through the door seams. She watched the plows, the lights, the winter itself, and asked me to buy an album—The Commodores. A song called "Still."

I sensed culture shock in her demeanor. That must be it, from the balmy weather in the Philippines to the frigid cold of the Missouri tundra.

The song selection seemed like an odd request until I dropped the needle at home. The music told a story I didn't want to hear: two people who had ignited once and then drifted, the flame tapering to a small, honest ember.

Maybe it had never been more than that. Perhaps I'd mistaken resistance for romance, distance for depth. I had asked God to sign off on my will and called it faith.

There was no comforting her. She wanted to be alone to think, to figure things out. I didn't have the words anyway.

That night, I left her in my apartment and drove to my parents' house through the same brutal weather. Somewhere on that road, I knew the end had already begun. And like too many times before, I turned up the noise and let it drown out the still small voice that was trying to tell me the truth.

Sail On

Three weeks later, I stood in the doorway of my bedroom and asked the question I'd been circling around in my mind: "Why did you come?" Regina sat on the edge of the bed, eyes down, then lifted the phone and spoke Tagalog to her sister in Colorado—soft, quick syllables I couldn't follow. The sound only sharpened my anger. I had staked everything on this. I had believed in mountains moving. All I'd done was chip at an iceberg.

My mother suggested we talk to a priest. Perfect, I thought. I'm trying to save a relationship, and now we're calling in clergy. Regina was Catholic and agreed. That tiny yes felt like a thread I could still hold.

The priest tamped tobacco into a pipe with careful fingers, lit it, and let the smoke curl between us. He listened, asked about paths and timing, about what we owed each other and ourselves. Then he turned to me and said,, "Do you want to work on this, or do you want to walk away?"

The answer rose before I could brace for it—clean, undeniable, flooding me with a relief that felt like air after a long dive.

"I want to walk away."

Something in the room exhaled. The earthquake that had been shaking my life had already dropped the bridge; there was nothing left to cross back to. Peace moved through me like a river. Regina said she wanted the same. The priest offered a kind, wandering benediction about how these moments can turn us, even toward a religious life someday. I wasn't in a spiritual mood. I wanted to sweep up my pieces and keep moving.

I bought her a ticket to Colorado. When I handed it to her, the weight I'd been carrying shifted off my shoulders.

My grandparents drove us to the airport in what felt like the longest car ride on record. At the gate, I said goodbye. I felt foolish, bruised, and not much wiser about God's will than when I started. Maybe this was what He kept trying to teach me: loss, and how to let go.

As she walked away, the sweetness of our first night together wouldn't come when I called for it. What I felt instead was a wild, guilty relief—like I'd just won a small, improbable lottery and been handed back my life.

Grandma Naomi, never a champion of a Filipina granddaughter-in-law, said, "We were all praying things would work out the way they were supposed to."

"I guarantee you they have," I said, rapping my knuckles on my grandfather's dashboard. "Drive on, sir. This is the first day of the rest of my life. All things, great and small, work together for good."

My grandfather barked a laugh. I laughed, too. Grandma shrugged from the back seat. I did feel good—lighter—and I believed those words, even if it would take years to understand them fully.

A few days later, I sprawled on my couch, letting the Commodores album spin long past "Still." I'd never made it to the last track. A lyric slipped into my ears, then hit me square in the chest. I sat up, stared at the turntable, nudged the needle back, and listened again. And then I laughed out loud and danced around my apartment like a teenager as the Lord hauled my heart up by the collar with a song Regina had unknowingly sent me to buy.

"Sail On" became my freedom song. I was twenty-five, one quarter of a century, still afloat. I endured a family wedding soon after, convinced every eye in the church was boring into my back. That was mostly in my head. It would be a long while before I loved like that again or trusted that way.

My faith didn't crumble; it grew. God kept reminding me life isn't an à la carte buffet where you order only what you want. Sometimes dreams limp, die, or never materialize. But when the room cleared out, Jesus stayed. That counted for more than I knew.

The Crossroads

By September 1980, I was staring down a full-time job and a stack of creative coursework, wondering how I could carry both. A thought came like a dare: Simplify your life and get on with it.

Still, small voice—or desperation? Too bold for panic, I think mainly because it worked.

I sold my '79 Grand LeMans, the one I'd bought when I came home from the military, back to the dealer, paid off the loan in cash, and walked the same lot to buy a blue '74 Ford LTD with 115,000 miles for a flat thousand. The vinyl bench seat was cracked, the AM radio hissed, and the speedometer wavered like a nervous hand. I let go of my $260-a-month apartment and climbed into a second-floor walkup for $90—a slanted floor, thin walls, and a stubborn radiator that wheezed to life at dusk.

I quit the full-time factory shift, took more hours at the college station, and loaded my schedule with classes. I traded bells and whistles for books and tapes. Morning smelled like burnt coffee and hot dust from the board; afternoons ticked to the clatter of the AP wire; nights were a red ON AIR light, splicing blocks, and the sweet snap of razor blades through magnetic tape. Over the next two years, the work lit a fuse in me I didn't know was there.

When I rolled up the gravel drive to my parents' farmhouse in the blue bomb, they came onto the porch and just stared. They listened while I laid out the plan. My mother looked at the car, at me, and I could see her thinking I'd gone plum loco—and, in a way, that Regina had pushed me there. She was right about the shake-up. Earthquakes rearrange the map. This one moved me where I needed to go.

On May 8, 1982, I crossed the stage at Northwest Missouri State University—broadcasting major, journalism minor—and stepped straight into another drought. A degree was one thing; a job in a recession was another. But this time, I was pared down, pointed, and moved.

And I knew how to keep going when the mountain didn't budge.

Reflections and Takeaways

This chapter chronicles a season of rupture and recalibration: a young broadcaster and former Marine navigating heartbreak, scarcity, and faith in the cold edges of Hobbs, New Mexico. What begins as a love story with Regina becomes an interior earthquake—one that topples illusions, exposes fault lines, and rearranges the map of the narrator's calling.

What Stands Out

- The juxtaposition of external cold (snow, wind, desert austerity) with internal disorientation underscores the chapter's emotional climate.
- Love is rendered not as a dramatic failure but as a clarifying force—ending becomes an act of truth-telling rather than defeat.
- Faith matures from miracle-seeking ("move the mountain") to resilient trust (showing up when the mountain doesn't move).

Central Themes

- Surrender vs. Control: The narrator learns the difference between asking God to endorse his will and actually listening.
- Loss as Catalyst: The breakup doesn't shatter him; it refines his life, sharpens his craft, and strengthens his faith.
- Calling Over Comfort: Trading a decent car and apartment for a beat-up Ford and a walk-up becomes the apprenticeship that births a vocation.

- Providence in the Ordinary: A priest's question, a Commodores record, and a blue LTD become unlikely instruments of grace.

Pivotal Moments

- The airport reunion's chilly distance—signaled by a ticket tapped on the head—shifts the narrative from romance to reckoning.
- The priest's blunt fork-in-the-road ("Work on it or walk away?") unlocks interior honesty and peace.
- "Sail On" transforming into a freedom anthem reframes grief as forward motion.
- Practical simplification (selling the car, moving apartments, reworking jobs) converts emotional clarity into disciplined action.

Spiritual Arc

- From triumphalism to trust: Faith grows not by getting desired outcomes but by discovering God's steady presence "when the room clears out."
- Discernment as subtraction: The call to "simplify your life" isn't austerity for its own sake; it's clearing the runway for purpose.

Key Takeaways

- Clarity often arrives at a loss before it feels like freedom.
- A closed door can be an invitation to simplify, focus, and recommit to your craft.

- Honest questions asked at the right moment can end an earthquake.
- Faith is less about moving mountains and more about walking faithfully when they don't move.
- Small, concrete steps (budget changes, schedule shifts) turn emotional insight into sustainable growth.

Questions for Further Reflection

- Where might you be asking for divine endorsement of your will rather than guidance?
- What could you simplify—today—to better serve your calling?
- Which "songs" (habits, voices, mentors) are shaping your story right now?
- What bridge has already dropped—and how might that be mercy, not failure?

This chapter doesn't glorify pain; it honors the truth that rupture can be redemptive. "Sail on" isn't escapism—it's discipleship with a steering wheel and a radio, choosing the long road of craft, character, and trust.

CHAPTER EIGHT
Aftershocks

"Life is about accepting challenges along the way, choosing to keep moving forward, and savoring the journey.

Roy T. Bennett

My youngest brother Karl arrived in 1976 while I was still serving in the Marine Corps, the last in my long line of younger siblings. Twenty-one years separated us in age.

By the time I finally held him, he'd grown from infant softness into a two-year-old whirlwind. As the oldest, I'd long since learned that responsibility isn't a jacket you take off; it's a skin you live in. God was shaping me in ways I didn't predict—teaching me that what happens is less decisive than how I answer it.

Leap of Faith, Thin Wallet

Following my broken engagement with Regina, I resigned from my factory job and poured myself into the last year and a half of school. Creativity erupted—finally, a fuse caught fire.

That fire cooled months after graduation. I filled the gap with an overnight security guard position. A short but sweet summer romance curtailed by circumstances beyond our control briefly filled the yearning in my heart for love.

When a radio DJ spot opened in Hobbs, New Mexico, 900-plus miles from home, I jumped. The Marine Corps had taught me to survive inside a system. Civilian life didn't come with rations or rules. Out here, every choice had a bill.

April of 1993 brought the job I wanted—and a paycheck that couldn't carry me. I miscalculated the move, the salary, and the cost of living. A headhunter had brokered it all, collecting ten percent of my first year's pay while I learned how far a dollar didn't go. Still, I hung on to faith and home. Letters from Mom stitched the miles smaller.

When the Letters Stopped

By September of '83, her letters went silent. I told myself it was nothing. Over the summer, when my parents visited, Mom asked for a kiss—unusual for our not-very-expressive family. Dad fidgeted at goodbye. I filed both under "overthinking" and pressed on.

Then one night in Hobbs, I warmed my hands against the wall heater as the phone rang. Mom's voice was bright, but I could hear tension buckling the edges—Grandma murmuring in the background, pauses stretching long.

Finally: "Marvin… Aunt Rachel died last week."

Sadness, a note of relief, then gratitude. MS had devoured Rachel's body but never her laughter. I remembered Uncle Edward wiping her mouth with a tenderness that told the truth about vows. Her suffering was over. I hung up, certain the strain in Mom's voice had an explanation. But the quiet after that call felt heavier than before.

Holiday Failures and a Frayed Faith

Hobbs began to nick at me. The cyst on my neck turned angry—impossible to ignore. Then came payday. The owner's wife pressed two twenties and a ten into my palm. "This is all we can pay at the moment." Gas would eat most of it. Rent would not get paid.

Two weeks prior, my boss had fronted me with cash for a new alternator. Promises were made about ad invoices "coming in next week. I started 1983 broke, hungry, and hoping for a miracle.

The doctor said the cyst needed surgery—and he wanted payment up front. No insurance. No cushion. Just pride and a thin wallet. I called home anyway.

My parents urged me to come home to regroup. They'd send money for the flight. The check arrived with a curt note from Mom: "Nineteen-eighty-four will be a new year. Prayers that it will be a better year for everyone."

The words rang like a warning bell. My mind filled the silence with worst-case scenarios. Trouble between my parents? Unthinkable—and somehow plausible. I called. Mom answered, voice tight.

"What are you calling for?"

"I was just wondering how everything is with you."

"I'm fine… Did you get the check?"

"Yes. I get the cyst removed on Friday."

"Good luck with that. I'm busy right now. We can talk when you get home."

The line went dead, and fear took its place.

The Cut and the Call

On the table, the surgeon numbed my neck and carved the intruder loose. I imagined him cutting away more than tissue, maybe the life I'd tried to build in Hobbs. When the Novocain wore off, pain throbbed hot and mean. I tossed on the couch that doubled as a bed and prayed.

The phone interrupted my pity party. Joan, my sister-in-law, didn't bother with preface. "Your mom has cancer."

The room tilted. I thought of the seven kids still at home. Cancer had already stolen from us—Orville, Anita, Donna—and it had claimed my best friend's leg while I was in the service. Joan said Mom's surgery was scheduled for the day of my flight. At DFW, I called for an update. "She came out of surgery about an hour ago, and everything went well," Joan said, brisk as a receptionist. No details. Just the long walk to the next gate.

Dad and my mother's parents met me at the airport. We had two hours in the car to speak the truth, and we didn't. I followed their lead—silence as a shield, as a prayer, as a dare. In the hospital parking lot, my grandparents slipped away. Dad turned the key, then turned to me.

"It's not good," he said. "It has spread too far. Doc gives her two months. Grandma and Grandpa are taking it hard. She doesn't know yet."

I nodded. There was nothing to say that wasn't a howl. Dad planned to stay at her bedside. I took the keys and headed home to the farmhouse, hoping morning would hand us something solid.

Laughter in the Kitchen

The house was loud before I even hit the porch. I rounded the short flight of stairs into the kitchen—same corner where I'd heard about my cousin's drowning years before—and froze, then laughed. Norbert, wearing a nightrobe, clung to one end of the oven light housing. Dean wrestled the other.

"Help," Norbert managed, shaking with laughter.

"What in the world?"

"Just help," he sputtered.

"You are a dork," Dean grinned, not letting up. "We were fighting, and Norbert slammed into it."

I moved to steady the fixture, and we all cracked up—the kind of laughter that knocks a little air back into your lungs. We weren't ready to cry yet. The aftershocks would have their say soon enough. That night, laughter built us a small shelter, just big enough for three brothers and a single fragile light.

Reflections and Takeaways

This chapter traces a passage from ambition to acute vulnerability: the eldest sibling chasing a radio dream in Hobbs while poverty tightens, illness intrudes, and family roles invert. What begins as a resume-building leap becomes a crucible of responsibility, humility, and faith—where silence around suffering is finally pierced by a phone call and, unexpectedly, by laughter in a farmhouse kitchen.

What Stands Out

- Eldest-child gravity: leadership by default—and later, by necessity—shapes choices and conscience.
- Calling vs. cost: passion for radio collides with hard math (low pay, no insurance, unstable employer).
- The ministry of letters: Mom's correspondence as a lifeline—and the dread when it stops.
- The shock of prognosis: "two months" reframes every priority in an instant.
- Laughter as refuge: comic chaos around an oven light becomes a pressure valve for grief.

Central Themes

- Response over circumstance: "It's not what happens, but how we respond" becomes lived theology.
- Humility in asking for help: calling home for money and medical support—pride surrendered to reality.
- The quiet of suffering: family silence as both protection and denial; truth finally spoken car-side.

- Faith under pressure: trust that endures through scarcity, sickness, and unanswered questions.
- Double burden of care: personal crisis (surgery) eclipsed by a parent's diagnosis—role reversal in real time.

Pivotal Moments

- Letters stop (Sept '83): the first tremor.
- "Aunt Rachel died": grief mixed with gratitude for release from MS.
- Cyst, no insurance, meager paycheck: precarity made plain.
- The note: "1984 will be a new year…"—ominous subtext.
- The call: "Your mom has cancer"—a sentence that redraws the map.
- The drive and disclosure: "It has spread… two months."
- Kitchen laughter with Norbert and Dean: joy threading its way through loss.

Key Takeaways

- Pay attention to absences: silence (stopped letters, flat tones) often speaks the loudest.
- Passion needs a plan: pair vocational leaps with sober financial/health safeguards.
- Ask sooner: seeking help early is wisdom, not failure.
- Hold two truths: it's human to feel both dread and relief, sorrow and laughter—at once.
- Lead by presence: in crisis, show up, listen, and share the load.

- Faith matures in limits: trust deepens when outcomes don't align with hopes.

Questions for Further Reflection

- Where might you be ignoring quiet signals that something is wrong?
- What practical supports (financial, medical, relational) do you need to put in place now?
- Who looks to you for steadiness—and how can you show up without self-erasure?
- What small practices help you hold both grief and joy without numbing either?

Final Note

This chapter doesn't romanticize hardship; it names it—and then shows how character is forged in the responses: a phone call made, a truth faced, a laugh shared. In the narrowing, a different kind of spaciousness appears as clarity, courage, and a faith that keeps choosing the next faithful step.

CHAPTER NINE
Responsibility Calls

"Honor your father and your mother, so that you may live long in the land the LORD your God is giving you."

EXODUS 20:12

We kept vigil under the fluorescent hush of St. Francis Hospital, a place where time stretched, and coffee soured in your mouth. I sat between my father and grandfather, three generations lined up as if to keep the past from slipping away. Grandpa's shoulders sagged. Tears pooled and clung to his lower lashes. My mother—his only surviving child—lay behind the door we were about to walk through, and grief had already found him.

"She doesn't know yet," my father said, jaw set, anger simmering behind his eyes. The doctor had told him not to tell her. My father wasn't made for silence or secrets.

"Is that right?" I asked. "How do you fight what you can't name?"

He exhaled hard. "I'm going to make him tell her. Today."

We filed in with our bravest smiles, my brother Vince and his wife, Joan; my maternal grandparents; Grandma Gertrude; and Dad leading us like a reluctant parade. Mom's eyes moved from face to face until they reached her father. She took one look at his tears and put her hand to her mouth. Truth doesn't always need words; sometimes it surfaces in a single look, a slight tremor. We had come to keep a secret. Grandpa had already told it with grief.

As we left the room, my father cursed the doctor beneath his breath, and I didn't stop him. We had tried to protect her. We failed. Maybe that was mercy.

"The doctor gave her two months," Dad said, as if daring the universe to contradict him.

We looked at each other and, without speaking, refused. If cancer was an enemy, then we would be at war.

Echoes of Loss

This wasn't my mother's first brush with cancer and overwhelming loss.

In 1982, we followed a funeral procession to Parnell Cemetery for Orville Durbin, my mother's cousin's husband. Leukemia had come like a thunderclap. Mom had folded into her hands in the Suburban and wept in a way that borrowed from other losses—Aunt Odelia in '69, my cousin Elmer's drowning in '63. I could still hear her whisper, "I can't believe we're here."

Two years later, I found myself thinking the same thing.

I believed in God, but He felt far away. I'd weathered storms before: a broken engagement four years back, a job that looked promising and then unraveled, a future that kept shifting like sand. Nothing about God's timing made sense to me. Yet my first thought when the diagnosis landed was practical and brutal: Who will finish raising my seven younger brothers and sisters? David was about to turn seventeen; Karl was seven. The gap between them felt like a chasm only Mom knew how to bridge.

1984, I decided, was going to be the year of miracles and thin faith. Maybe one fed the other.

The Ask

Once Mom was moved to a room, I stood at her bedside with Dad. He spoke with a softness that surprised me—like the young man who had farmed nine years with Grandpa George and then found the courage to claim his independence.

"You said things weren't working out in Hobbs," Mom whispered.

"Not exactly," I said, trying to sound steadier than I felt. "The radio station might not survive. I'm…in a rut."

Dad cleared his throat. "We're going to need help. I can co-sign a loan to get you back home." He paused. "Or you could look for another job."

The proud man I knew was asking for help. He was turning to his oldest son to help carry the house, the chores, the homework, the dinners, the arguments, the curfews, the chaos. I was twenty-eight and not where I wanted to be. Coming home felt like a detour from my own life. But I could feel the rightness of it gathering in my chest like a tide.

I looked at Mom. "What do you think I should do?"

She only nodded—one slight, steady movement. It was enough. Decision made—Goliath named and two months thrown over our shoulders.

The war had begun.

Operation Deep Clean

Back on the farmstead, my aunts swept in with mops, vacuums, and casseroles. Operation Deep Clean, we called it—some homegrown ritual of healing where lemon cleaner and laughter tried to disinfect fear. Cancer had never nested in the Wilmes backyard before. We didn't know the rules, so we did the next right thing: we scrubbed, we cooked, we showed up.

Watching from just beyond our circle was Father Regis, the priest who once woke a sleepy parish when he stood at Orville's funeral and declared: "It is not over!" His voice had rolled through the church like a drumbeat, and something in me had answered, even if my mind didn't yet know how.

Dad and I had our own war—over faith. He loved order and disliked my brand of Jesus-talk. To him, the God I'd found felt like wishful thinking—the religion of the me generation. Sundays growing up, he'd pass me the Sunday Visitor, pipe smoke curling between us, and say, "Read this." I'd take the liberal view, he'd take the conservative, and we'd argue until my face flushed and Mom played referee, reminding us that we believed the same things—just took different roads to get there.

In time, my life braided my born-again experience with my cradle Catholic roots. If Christ were at the center, we would be closer than we thought. It would take years to understand the fullness I eventually found in the Church. For now, what I knew was this: God doesn't leave us where He finds us.

And priests aren't spared deserts. Father Regis had become Mom's friend through the parish catechism program. He would suffer this with us, too.

Ice and flooding

As Mom recovered from surgery, I packed to return to Hobbs long enough to resign and come home for good. The word metastasized hung in the air like a storm front: colon cancer, spread to the liver. The ostomy bag told its own hard truth. My aunts said that for Christmas, Mom had given out statuettes of the Virgin Mary—each with a single tear on the right cheek. A quiet signal. A whisper she could send without saying anything at all.

If there had been a two-month clock, it would have fallen behind a dresser somewhere and stopped ticking. We weren't counting down; we were gearing up. Seven kids at home will do that for a mother. They become the cause and the cure, the fight and the finish line.

I flew into Midland, Texas, and drove my dark blue '74 LTD a hundred miles to Hobbs, skating more than moving across the roads glazed with ice. That old Ford had carried me through plenty—a renewal of purpose, more than a few long prayers.

I'd been in a storm like this once before, years back, weaving through mountain roads with a rental car after visiting a buddy at the Yuma base. The interstate had closed; trucks jackknifed; I crawled forward at twenty, speaking to God because no one else could hear me, and this was before the world carried phones in its pockets.

Out of nowhere, a phone booth appeared—tucked into a turn as if God had folded it into the mountain. I called the Camp Pendleton base, where I was being discharged from. "I'll be late," I told the sergeant. He said to be safe. Of course, he believed me—who lies their way into a delay on discharge day?

Now, rolling off the Texas ice into my Hobbs driveway, I felt the same mix of relief and exhaustion. I heard it before I saw it—the hiss and gurgle, like a stream under the house. Only there was no stream. I unlocked the door and found water spraying from the kitchen sink like a busted artery. The pipes had frozen and burst. Floors slick, boxes soaked, a week's worth of ruin on repeat.

I stood there and laughed—wild, sacrilegious laughter that came from some cracked place inside me. "Anything else?" I called up to the ceiling. "Anything else?" Silence met sarcasm, as it often does. And yet I felt a small, inexplicable steadiness settle on me, the kind you get when you're past the point of fear.

Grace, maybe.

I shut off the water, called the landlord, and waded through the mess. He admitted he knew the pipes were trouble. He assumed I'd call if I needed help. "I was gone a week," I said, rubbing my temples. Then I mopped, cursed under my breath, and prayed the oldest prayer I know. "Lord, get me out of this pit."

Corrie Ten Boom's line from The Hiding Place rose like a rope that had been tossed into a well: There is no pit so deep that He is not deeper still.

"Yes, Lord," I said, wringing out a towel over the sink. "But how deep do you want me to go?"

Maybe that's what 1984 was—depth training. Not the year Mom hoped for. Not easy. But honest. The kind that carves you out and leaves room for something more substantial than fear to move in.

Back home, we shifted from vigil to campaign. Appointments. Treatments. Meals timed around nausea. Hope hanging on the ordinary—the way sunlight hit the kitchen table at four, the sound of my brothers and sisters wrestling upstairs, the small satisfaction of a swept floor, a steady breath.

We had no guarantees, only the work. Still, in the quiet, I could hear it again, the line Father Regis boomed across our parish during a winter funeral: It is not over.

I chose to believe him.

Reflections and Takeaways

Truth vs. protection: The family's attempt to shield Mom from her prognosis collides with a more profound truth—grief can't be disguised. Grandpa's tears say what words won't. The chapter wrestles with the ethics of withholding information versus honoring a patient's agency.

- Refusing the script: The doctor's "two months" becomes the antagonist's line, the family collectively rejects. The shift from shock to resolve reframes illness from fate to fight.
- Duty as calling: The narrator's detour home—away from career dreams—reads less like surrender and more like vocation. Love asks for sacrifice, purpose answers.
- Community care as liturgy: "Operation Deep Clean" is more than housekeeping—it's a ritual of solidarity. Practical acts (cleaning, cooking, showing up) become sacraments of hope.
- Faith under strain and in motion: God feels silent; the heart keeps reaching. The refrain "It is not over!" threads a theology of resurrection through ordinary suffering. Faith is shown as a long arc—born-again zeal meeting cradle-Catholic depth, with desert seasons for priests and laypeople alike.
- Resilience through dark humor: The burst pipes scene—wild laughter amid ruin—reveals crisis as a crucible for grit. The Corrie Ten Boom line ("no pit so deep…") anchors despair to promise.
- Symbols that speak: The Virgin Mary statuettes with a single tear, an ostomy bag, a surprise mountain phone

booth—ordinary objects become signposts of grief, body-reality, and providence.

- Intergenerational friction and love: Father–son debates sharpen conviction but end in shared core beliefs; Mom is the reconciling center. Difference doesn't preclude devotion.
- The ordinary as anchor: Treatment brings a cadence: meals, chores, sun on the kitchen table. Hope is sustained by small, dependable rhythms.
- Family metamorphosis: Crisis is a catalyst. The family moves from insulation to advocacy, from deference to doctors to engaged, questioning partners in care.

Human and ethical insights

- Patient autonomy matters: Withholding a terminal diagnosis, however well-intended, risks disempowering the person most affected. Compassion and honesty are allies, not rivals.
- Advocacy is learned: The chapter documents a shift from "doctor knows best" to "we have a voice." That evolution becomes part of the family's courage.
- Grief's language is embodied: Tears, posture, tone—these speak before policy and plans. Please pay attention to what bodies tell us when words hesitate.

Spiritual takeaways

- Faith is both confession and practice: Lament, prayer, scripture, and shared rituals sustain when certainty fades.

- Paradox of presence: God may feel absent, yet grace shows up as steadiness, timely help, or a phone booth on a mountain road.
- Resurrection as stance: "It is not over!" becomes more than a sermon line; it's a way of walking through the valley.

Questions this chapter invites

- When is truth-telling the deepest mercy, and how do we do it well?
- How does a family discern roles without erasing anyone's dreams?
- What practices sustain faith when God seems silent?
- What does patient-centered advocacy look like in real time?
- How do symbols (tears, statuettes, a phrase) shape communal courage?

Personal applications

- Build small, steady rituals during crisis—meals, walks, sunlight, shared readings.
- Name the fight and the limits; let honesty empower choices.
- Invite community help as a discipline, not a last resort.
- Keep a "grace log": note surprising provisions, however ordinary.
- Hold space for both lament and laughter—they can coexist without canceling each other out.

This chapter is about moving from shock to agency, from secrecy to solidarity, from thin faith to tried faith. It argues, in story-form, that while prognosis can set parameters, love, community, and honest faith determine the posture—and sometimes, that posture changes everything. "It is not over" becomes less a slogan and more a way to keep walking.

CHAPTER TEN
The Crucifix

"I consider that our present sufferings are not worth comparing with the glory that will be revealed in us. For the creation waits in eager expectation for the children of God to be revealed. For the creation was subjected to frustration, not by its own choice, but by the will of the one who subjected it, in hope that the creation itself will be liberated from its bondage to decay and brought into the freedom and glory of the children of God."

ROMANS 8:18-21

The crucifix pinned to my mother's clothing became a constant in a year when nothing else was. It clung to her bathrobe, nightgown, and blouses, catching light and breath with every step she took. By then, it wasn't just jewelry; it was testimony. Her faith was stitched into her days, and that crucifix—plain, steady, unpretentious—was the thread holding them together.

Returning to my childhood home felt like stepping into a story I wasn't ready to read. Hobbs, New Mexico, still clung to my clothes in the smell of dust and distant radio jingles, but northwest Missouri was home, and home was where the sickness was. My rediscovery of Catholicism had begun as a quiet ember. Still, now it flickered against the wind of perfectionism—my mistaken belief that God wanted me polished before He'd meet me in my mess. He didn't. He met me on the farmhouse porch.

I was halfway up the walk when she jumped from around the corner.

"Boo."

It wasn't the joke that startled me. It was her face—no longer drained by the hospital's gray light but bright with some fierce, anchored joy. She'd always had this way of looking at you like life would be okay because she knew something you didn't. In that moment, I believed her.

Inside, cards and letters had taken over the house. Stacks of envelopes—handwriting from every direction—leaned against lamps, were tucked into bowls, and slid between books. People she had helped and comforted in quiet ways were now sending their voices back to her: stories, prayers, pieces of Scripture, clippings with folded edges. She had touched so many lives that the mail looked like a topographical map of her kindness.

Buried among the notes was a letter from a young priest named Father John. He'd visited and left a small package—a crucifix—and his story.

"I was given this crucifix at a crucial crossroads in my own life," he wrote. "The person who gave it to me received it when he was in crisis. He encouraged me to pass it on when I found someone who needed it more."

He had kept it until his own storm cleared. Then he paid it forward, as promised.

And now it was my mother's.

I found myself wondering what brought him to his knees—what doubt, what loss—but I didn't need the details to understand the weight of his gift. The chain was thin, the cross simple. But meaning isn't measured in metal. A crucifix isn't meant to be pretty; it's meant to be true. Our traditions keep Christ on the cross not because we deny the resurrection, but because we remember the road to it. Jesus said, "Deny yourself. Pick up your cross and follow me." We rush past that sentence as if discipleship were a sprint to an empty tomb. But the road to dawn runs through a hill called Golgotha.

What astonished me most wasn't the crucifix itself; it was my mother's fidelity to it. She wore it like one wears breath. When she bent to tie a shoe, it swung. When she laughed, it danced. When pain came, it rested still against her chest. It became her witness—her hand raised on the stand of suffering, testifying that hope is real.

By then, cancer had taken up residence in our home. On paper, the facts were cold: it had spread to her liver. In life, the facts burned. My parents did everything the family doctor recommended, but as a family, we were undereducated about the disease—about stages, protocols, and specialists. Back then, cancer was a single bleak word to me. I didn't yet know it was a maze requiring both courage and a map.

"Don't worry," she'd say. "I will beat this." She meant it. She had to. Seven children were still under her roof. She couldn't imagine God granting their births without also granting her the strength to raise them.

Aunt Dee, who was more like a big sister than an aunt, would later tell me that my abrupt departure from my first radio job in New Mexico had been a mercy disguised as a disappointment. "If it had been wonderful," she said, "it wouldn't have been easy to leave. God had a plan. It wasn't time for your career to work out—your parents needed you now." I didn't yet know her full faith story, but I trusted her. We'd grown up together, after all—her showing me, what steady looked like, me looking up to her with the kind of respect that never quite leaves.

My parents were a team. Mom had long been the heartbeat of our home, and in recent years, once Roland and Karl started school, she'd become a pillar in our parish—reliable, wise, endlessly willing. That's why nuns, priests, and laypeople flowed toward her bedside when the news broke. Among them: Father John and his crucifix.

The crossroads

Almost a month after the diagnosis, I drove Mom to see our family doctor. She was hoping for a referral to a radiologist. Dad met us in town because he'd taken another car for servicing. Even then, Mom prized her independence; she went in alone while I idled in the car, the radio mumbling news and songs I didn't really hear. I didn't know better. Our roles had always been clear: she supported us. We didn't know how to support her yet.

When she returned, she didn't speak at first. She gripped the steering wheel, breathed, then turned to me. Her voice trembled, but her eyes were flint.

"We have to go get your father."

The way she said "your father" told me something had broken.

"What happened?"

Her composure cracked, just a little. "He asked if I'd started taking pain pills yet." She blinked back tears. "Can you believe it? He's already given up."

The cruelty landed slowly, then all at once. In that sterile room, a sentence had been handed to her like a prescription for surrender. But something rose in her, in us—instinct, love, revolt—and that same day we sought a second opinion. We drove past pride, past habit, past the comfort of what we knew, and headed toward St. Luke's Hospital in Kansas City, Missouri. That day, we reclaimed her care. That day, we insisted on more than two months. That day, we learned that time—real time, hope-filled time—is worth more than gold.

Pride ruins more than reputations; it endangers lives. Our family doctor—the same man who had delivered Vince and me—was fired that afternoon. He'd been so tangled in his own guilt over missing the cancer during prior surgery that he couldn't bring himself to hand Mom's case to an oncologist. Maybe he feared a lawsuit. Perhaps he was ashamed. But his pride wasn't ours to bear. We walked away.

With Mom's faith as our compass, we didn't let bitterness become our god. She led us in forgiveness—as fiercely and hard-won as any battle. I struggled with blame; I won't lie about that. But she lived the kind of quiet sainthood that makes accusation feel small.

By then, I was in my seventh year of conversion, and Satan knew where to press. Would my faith hold under the weight? Would I trust God not as an idea but as a lifeline? Some days the answer was yes. Other days it was simply the crucifix against her collarbone, warm from her skin, reminding me that love meets suffering with presence, not platitudes.

I think of Father John's letter often—the way one act of kindness can become a lineage. Someone once reached out to him. He reached out to Mom. Mom reached back to everyone who loved her with courage that made us braver. The crucifix moved from hand to hand, life to life, because the cross itself has always been a story of passing on: mercy received, mercy given.

If you ask me what changed that year, I could give you dates and doctors, hospital floors, and challenging conversations. But what I remember most is simple: the sound of a small chain when my mother turned her head; the way light gathered on a worn metal Christ; the steadiness of a woman who believed—not that suffering wouldn't come, but that it wouldn't get the last word.

We picked up our cross and followed. And somehow, there was grace enough for the road.

Reflections and Takeaways

This chapter is a tender meditation on faith under fire, the quiet heroism of a mother, and the hard-won wisdom born from crisis. A simple crucifix becomes the thread that ties suffering, community, courage, and grace together.

Big Takeaways

- Faith is embodied: A crucifix worn daily becomes not an ornament but a witness—suffering and hope held together.
- God meets us where we are: Perfectionism gives way to presence; grace finds us in the mess, not after we've tidied it.
- Community matters: Letters and prayers map the reach of a life lived generously; love returns when we need it most.
- Advocacy saves lives: A second opinion can reclaim time, dignity, and possibility; humility in medicine is essential.
- Forgiveness is strength: Letting go of blame protects the heart, even as it sets boundaries and seeks better care.
- Roles can shift: The caregiver becomes the one cared for; the family learns new ways to show up.
- Grace is contagious: The "pay-it-forward" crucifix turns one person's consolation into a lineage of courage.
- Discipleship includes the cross: We don't rush to resurrection; we walk through Golgotha with Christ and each other.

What This Chapter Teaches About Faith

- Faith is not denial of suffering—it's companionship through it.

- Symbols matter when they're lived: the crucifix is a daily yes to love amid pain.
- Spiritual maturity includes surrendering perfectionism and receiving help.
- Hope is both declaration ("I will beat this") and discipline (showing up, forgiving, asking for more).

What This Chapter Teaches About Care and Advocacy

- Ask for specialists early—complex illness demands expert eyes.
- Don't let a clinician's pride or fear block appropriate referrals.
- Firing a doctor can be an act of love and stewardship.
- Advocacy is a family ministry: someone sits in, takes notes, asks questions, and pursues options.

Practice: Putting the Insights to Work

For caregivers:

- Sit in on appointments, take notes, and request written summaries.
- Prepare 3–5 key questions before each visit.
- Track symptoms, meds, and side effects in a shared log.
- Normalize second opinions—especially for serious diagnoses.

For communities/parishes:

- Organize letter-writing, meal trains, and prayer chains.
- Create "companions for appointments"—trained volunteers to accompany patients to medical visits.

- Share sacramentals or symbols of hope with a "pass-it-on" tradition.

For patients:

- Claim both agency and rest: it's okay to ask, to change doctors, and to say "I need help."
- Wear or carry what reminds you you're not alone (a cross, a prayer, a note).
- Define a "care circle" of 3–4 people with specific roles.

Reflection and Journal Prompts

- Where have I confused perfection with holiness? How might I let God meet me as I am?
- What symbol or practice helps me carry hope when words fail?
- Is there a place in my life where I need a "second opinion"—medical, spiritual, or vocational?
- Who needs a letter, a visit, or a small sign of solidarity from me this week?
- How can I forgive without minimizing harm—holding both boundary and mercy?

A Small Rule of Life Inspired by the Chapter

- Wear or carry one reminder of hope daily.
- Speak one encouragement each morning.
- Ask one brave question in every critical meeting.
- Practice one act of mercy each week.
- End the day with one breath of gratitude.

Closing Thought

This chapter shows that love is strongest when its simplest: a cross around a mother's neck, a letter passed from hand to hand, a son deciding not to give up. Suffering doesn't get the last word; faithful presence does. And sometimes, the holiest thing we can do is ask for help—and then pass the hope along.

CHAPTER ELEVEN
Cancer Support

"A lesson for all of us is that for every loss, there is victory, for every sadness, there is joy, and when you think you have lost everything, there is hope."

GERALDINE SOLON

The first night June Owen said, "In all sadness, there is joy; in all joy, there is sadness," the room went quiet enough to hear the coffee burn. A simple line, but it tilted the table we were sitting around. I carried that paradox out into the parking lot and have carried it ever since.

By early 1984, our house had become a small country of crisis. We were learning a new language: oncology appointments, scans, side effects, options. A weekly cancer support group at the local hospital became one of our few steady rhythms.

June led the circle with a steady voice and a soft box of tissues near her elbow. Mom went when she could, until simply sitting in a chair was too much. My brother and his wife came at first, but two small children and bedtime battles prevailed. My grandparents—eighty-three and seventy-eight, loyal and fragile—tried once. They couldn't sit in a bright room and name the dark without crying. It wasn't their way.

The group was part classroom, part chapel: facts and figures one minute, hard-won testimonies the next. Dad found ballast in it. Mom did not. She was never one to center herself, especially in a way that might burden anyone else.

"Does it make you angry?" June asked her.

Mom looked around the table as if taking attendance of every face. Maybe because her parents were there, perhaps because she was who she'd always been, she only shrugged. "No, I'm not angry."

The small gold crucifix on her blouse caught the light when she said it. I remembered that summer afternoon the year before—her asking me for a kiss, something she never asked for, and the way my heart broke with the simple request. If she was angry, she would never let us see it. Her life had always been about the rest of us. Even now she was thinking about how we were taking this.

June passed a purple deck across the table. "The Un Game," she said, smiling. "Icebreakers."

I drew a card. What is your worst fear?

Mom and I locked eyes. She smiled like we had already agreed on the answer in a private language forged by years of letters while I was away in the military.

"My biggest fear is that I will lose my mother to cancer," I said.

The words clattered on the table. For a second, mouths fell open, and eyes shifted. Mom only nodded. In that moment, an advocate took his first breath. I stopped being a quiet observer and stepped into the role that had been waiting: caregiver, reporter, encourager. I would sit in this circle and tell them what was happening to

Mom—the steps forward and the setbacks. I would learn more than I wanted to know about the process and about myself.

Life's cruelties can break you. They can also make you stronger still.

Driving Ms. Peggy

The second opinion at St. Luke's, with Dr. Munson, refined the plan: five weeks of daily radiation. Kansas City was two hours each way. Mom refused to stay there. She wanted her home, her kids, her people.

The planting season was starting. Dad had fields to put in the ground. We decided I would drive.

Mornings began in the half-light. A thermos of coffee on the counter. The creak of the screen door. Gravel popped under the tires until we met the smooth line of the highway. Sometimes we rode with the radio low; sometimes in the quiet hum of the engine and the kind of silence only mothers and sons can keep together.

At the hospital, the radiation machine's arm arced like a slow metal halo. Someone had taped a picture of Tom Selleck to its side—an odd, merciful distraction. Mom joked about having Magnum, P.I. watch over her. Humor makes a thin bridge, but we crossed it daily.

The treatment itself took less than an hour. Then the long drive home. Past fields not yet green. Past towns with a single blinking light. We measured time in mile markers and follow-up appointments. It was May now—nearly five months since her diagnosis—and we were living one day at a time, because looking much farther was a way of falling.

In April, we'd celebrated Mom and Dad's thirtieth anniversary at the American Legion in Parnell, and for one afternoon, the town turned out, and joy had the louder voice. In the photos, her smile was radiant and unruined. The truth was that the tumor had been growing. Sitting hurt. Without the radiation, the pain would have become a sentence. But we were in a necessary denial then, holding a future we could not bear to name, and believing—fiercely—that we would find a cure.

The community, hearing the same whisper we tried to outrun, fed us with casseroles and cards. Church families showed up with hot meals night after night. Mom stopped going to Mass when the pews became an enemy. She kept the portable phone by her bed like a lifeline to the world. Her world had shrunk to that room, and still she found ways to fill it with grace.

I picked up a weekend overnight shift at a Christian radio station in Shenandoah, fifty miles northwest. Three nights a week. It wasn't conducive to a social life, but I was not accepting applications for one. The programming fed me. Sitting in that booth with the red ON AIR light glowing, I longed for Christ's nearness the way a field longs for rain.

A benefit was held for our family. At the kitchen table afterward, Dad slid the envelope across to me. "Use it," he said. "You've put your life on hold for us." I was honored, humbled, and a little undone. I used the funds to buy new tires and converted a six-month note into a loan I could manage. Small mercies—rubber on the road, stability in the ledger—add up. Life wasn't perfect that summer. But it was good.

The call to service

God had been forming something in me since childhood—a tenderness for the underdog, a habit of listening. In the service, guys came to me with their messes and asked if I could help untangle them. In

1984, Dad started doing the same. The walls between father and son came down. We stood side by side, hands in the same work, hearts on the same line.

I was single, and some nights that felt like its own kind of ache. But if I hadn't been single, I don't know that I could have come home. I don't know if the choices would have been mine to make so quickly or so freely. The truth is, they wouldn't have been.

A priest had hinted, back in 1980 when my engagement fell apart, that maybe it was a sign—maybe God was calling me to the priesthood. Father Regis said something similar that spring. I tried the thought on like a suit coat that didn't quite fit around the shoulders.

Would I have been able to help if I were married, already planted in a career? No. That answer arrived plain as day.

I prayed that God would use me to help my siblings find their footing in a complex world. Looking back decades later, I see that prayer as something given to me, not something I invented. Maybe the Holy Spirit had a hand on my back, guiding the words before I knew what they'd cost.

The road in those years kept curving into detours, and I kept trying to drive it straight. I did not yet understand the process—how leaning not on my own understanding and trusting that all things work together is not a pretty slogan but a discipline. Still, a quiet strength met me each morning. Some of it was birth order—the oldest shouldering what the oldest shoulders. Some of it was co-dependence, perhaps. Some of it was simply love.

I had to answer the priesthood question honestly. In 1984, I turned it over and finally set it down. God wasn't calling me to the collar. He was calling me to be single for the moment—no less holy, no less necessary, just different. The loss of my engagement had not been the end of a story; it had been the opening to another.

To come home fully, I knew I had to go back to Confession, a door I hadn't opened since high school. St. Gregory's offered a Reconciliation prayer service. Priests sat on steel chairs scattered throughout the nave. Another chair faced each one—confessor and penitent in the open, near occupied pews. The "new church," they called it.

I sat down anyway. The noise rose and fell like the weather. Privacy felt like old currency no longer spent. I rushed through a litany years long, the priest nodding, absolving, sending me out with a small penance and a larger relief. I left with hesitancy, yes, but also with desire. My issues were with the church in places, not with God. God, I suspected, had a longer list of issues with me than I had with Him.

And yet, even that thought made me smile. If all sadness carries a seam of joy, perhaps even my stubbornness was stitched to grace.

We drove back and forth to Kansas City until the calendar said stop. We measured victories in inches, losses in whispers, faith in the getting up again. The paradox held: grief braided with gladness, the dark laced with light. And I, who feared the unthinkable, kept choosing the next faithful thing—one mile marker at a time.

Reflections and takeaways

Core takeaways

- Paradox as ballast: The chapter lives inside the tension that grief and grace can co-exist—and sometimes strengthen each other.
- Caregiving is a calling: Advocacy is born the moment the narrator speaks his worst fear aloud. Service becomes identity, not just duty.
- Community matters: Casseroles, cards, a benefit envelope—small mercies that make the long haul survivable.
- Necessary denial: "One day at a time" isn't evasion; it's a survival strategy when the future is unbearable to name.
- Faith as practice, not platitude: Scripture ("lean not on your own understanding") and sacrament (Confession) ground the narrator's resilience.
- Vocation redefined: Singleness is honored as a legitimate, even providential, calling—no less meaningful than priesthood or marriage.
- Generational limits: Different family members support in different ways; not all spaces (like the support group) fit all temperaments or eras.
- Boundaries and burdens: The narrator suspects co-dependence even as he shoulders what the eldest often does—an honest nod to the complexity of love.

Moments that linger

- The Un Game card: "What is your worst fear?" — Naming the unthinkable catalyzes purpose.
- The crucifix on Mom's blouse: A quiet symbol of a faith that refuses to center anger.
- Driving Ms. Peggy: Two hours each way, Tom Selleck taped to the radiation arm—humor as a thin but sturdy bridge.
- The anniversary party: Radiance in photos against a body's hidden suffering—joy not as denial, but defiance.
- The kitchen-table envelope: Dad's trust and gratitude made tangible—love speaking in pragmatics.
- Confession on steel chairs: Vulnerability in the open—imperfect ritual still mediating grace.

Faith and meaning

- Prayer as gift: The narrator reframes a past prayer as Spirit-led, recasting his role from volunteer to steward.
- Process over answers: Trust becomes a daily practice, not a solved equation.
- Redemptive reframing: Loss (a broken engagement) becomes the opening for a different kind of calling and presence.

Gentle insights for readers on similar roads

- Name the fear safely: Speaking it can convert dread into direction.

- Accept help early: Let casseroles, rides, and small funds be grace, not guilt.
- Build thin bridges: Humor, ritual, music, and routine can carry heavy loads.
- Preserve the person: Keep preferences central (home vs. hospital) to honor dignity.
- Hold both truths: Practice the "paradox posture"—room for grief and gratitude at once.

Questions for reflection or discussion

- Where in your life have you experienced joy braided into sadness?
- What simple practices (drive, prayer, music, meals) keep you steady in crisis?
- Which roles do you assume by habit (oldest child, fixer, protector)? Where do they serve you—and where do they cost you?
- How do you distinguish calling from expectation?
- What symbols or small mercies helped you feel carried when life felt too large?

This chapter shows that while illness narrows circumstances, love—and the daily, disciplined hope it demands—can widen meaning, mile by mile.

CHAPTER TWELVE

Crisis of Faith

"To everything there is a season, and a time to every purpose under the heaven: A time to be born, and a time to die; a time to plant, and a time to pluck up that which is planted; A time to kill, and a time to heal; a time to break down, and a time to build up: A time to weep, and a time to laugh; a time to mourn, and a time to dance; A time to cast away stones, and a time to gather stones together; a time to embrace, and a time to refrain from embracing; A time to get, and a time to lose; a time to keep, and a time to cast away."

ECCLESIASTES 3: 1-6

The radiation did its work—not the miracle cure my mother had prayed for, but enough to shrink the tumor and quiet the pain. From her bed, she still ran the household with that gentle authority only a mother can muster, issuing instructions like whispered prayers. Near the end of treatment, she scratched her forearm and sighed, "I don't know what it means, but I itch like crazy."

"Maybe that's a good sign," I offered.

"I'm just going to believe it is," she said, and then tucked the worry away.

People called. They always insisted they didn't want to bother her. I insisted they did. She needed those voices—their fussing and sweetness—to tether her to the world beyond the bedroom door.

I lived the summer as fully as I could. The radio station kept my mind occupied and a little money coming in. At home, I helped keep the gears turning while my sisters, Linda and Nancy, surrendered pieces of their childhood to chores that asked more of them than any summer ever should.

One afternoon, Mom made a quiet declaration. She came into the living room in a shirt and shorts and sat in her chair. When I walked downstairs and saw her, I stopped cold. Her body was a whisper. How had she hidden so much loss beneath her clothes and smile? We had grown skilled at not naming the elephant in the room. That silence—somehow—was part of how we survived.

In August, we threw her a fifty-first birthday—two, actually. One at the farm with Dad's family, and another at the park with Mom's side. We laughed; we ate; we pretended time would stretch. But by mid-September, she grew sick again, and we drove her to St. Luke's Hospital in Kansas City. In and out, out and in—admitted, released, admitted again. Finally, Dr. Munson called my father and me aside.

"There is nothing more we can do for Peggy," he said. "I recommend transferring her to your local hospital. I'm sorry."

We nodded, as people do when the earth tilts beneath them. I understood but refused to let the truth weigh on my chest. My denial ran fathoms deep. Still, the words "local hospital" rang like a bell I couldn't unhear. Sending her home meant sending her home to die.

My faith, meanwhile, wobbled like a loose mast in heavy wind. I was afraid to believe in anything good, fearful that if I did and nothing good happened, then God might not be real.

The same God I had cursed at thirteen had promised to be with me until the end of the age. Through storms and squalls, He'd steadied my boat. But now the waves were high again. She had been declared beyond hope back in January; somehow, we stood at the edge of October. I told myself she wouldn't die. I clung to technicalities and doctors' hedges and word choices and miracles I had not seen.

On that ground, God began to deal with me—plainly, insistently. Two years ago, Father Regis had sent me soaring with his "It is not over" at a funeral. Now I was on a collision course with the same priest, who would ask me to face a truth I didn't want to name.

I kept hearing talk of "God's will." How could this be God's will?

My father's maternal aunt and uncle—no children of their own, forged in hard knocks and steeped in an old, sturdy Catholic faith—stood by Mom's bed and spoke a language that felt foreign. Aunt Rose clasped Mom's thin hand and whispered, "God will use your sufferings to give salvation to your children."

Foreign words to me, because I was still speaking the language of my will.

There was so much I didn't know. I didn't know the conversations my parents had in the barren years between my brother Vince and David, when my mother—an only child—longed for more children. "My prayers will never be answered," she once told my father, head resting against his chest.

"My dear," he said, "if God wants you to have more children, He will answer."

Who had the greater faith? My father, raised Catholic and steady in belief? My mother, caught between questions and longing, was raised in a home divided by religion. I thought about my maternal grandmother's wrestling with God. "I did everything you asked," I imagine her saying. "Still, my boys died. You gave me only a daughter. Why?" Perhaps the ensuing silence made stepping into faith more difficult for her. She attended church with Grandpa Roy but stayed unbaptized—until my mother, persistent and prayerful, nudged her across the line.

At seventy-eight, during the 1982 Easter Vigil, Naomi Tuttle was baptized. At the very moment the water touched her, a lightning bolt cracked outside our small Parnell parish. My mother always called it God's answer. She turned to us, beaming, as if heaven itself had underlined her prayer.

Where was that lightning now?

Our family doctor had never sat us all down to chart the terrain ahead. Instead, he shouldered the responsibility alone and decided—for us—what despair or hope should look like. After he saw that the cancer had spread to her liver, he did not refer her to an oncologist. He withdrew from the fight; my mother had not consented to quit. That was his mistake. He underestimated her resolve and decided what was best without her input. The cancer would not vanish on its own. And yet the radiation did what it could: not a cure, but a gift of time—a summer's worth of days in which she lived fully and said her long goodbye. She never surrendered to the black hole of unbelief.

I did.

My crisis of faith was selfish; everything bent toward me. In all sadness, there is joy; in all joy, sadness. Mom knew this. She was teaching it with her life and her crucifix—the one she wore daily, a quiet proclamation of trust. Her doctor had declared her beyond hope. She refused that verdict and rose above it. Her courage helped the rest of us maintain denial, yes, but it also bore witness to something larger, something holy.

After she was admitted to St. Francis in Maryville, we kept vigil—Dad, his mother, Mom's parents, my brother and his wife, and me. People streamed in. Many I'd never met. All of them had been touched by my mother's kindness somewhere along the way. Dad believed that if a miracle were going to happen, it would. I thought each day we were given was a miracle in itself. Mom kept talking about going home. A Baptist minister prayed over her, telling her she'd be ready for whichever home the Lord called her to—this one or the next. She smiled and nodded.

One afternoon, we were alone when she glanced over her left shoulder toward the wall. "Hear that?" she asked.

"What?" I said, following her gaze. "Hear what?"

"Water," she whispered. A soft smile lifted her face as she let her head rest back on the pillow.

A waterfall rose in my mind, cool, clean, endless. I don't know what she saw or heard. I only know peace entered the room with it.

I had never watched a person die. We were unprepared. Dad and I held each other up and looked forward as best we could. Only years later did I learn Mom's talk of home wasn't about heaven at all. It was the house with the kids in it—the ones she had begged God for. He had answered. She wanted to go to them. Why couldn't she?

During the second week in Maryville, I met Father Regis at the hospital entrance just after he'd given Mom the Anointing of the Sick. His face was grave; his voice, deliberate.

"I'm so sorry for you and your family," he said. "Marvin, you must hand her over to the Lord now. You must let her go."

I stared at the man in black as if he were a stranger. Was this the same priest who'd inflamed my faith at Orville Durbin's funeral? Now it seemed all these men could talk about was death—as if they were eager for the dirt to settle on my mother's grave.

"We still have hope," I shot back.

"There is no place for false hope," he said gently.

I turned away, angry and unmoored, and later called my sister-in-law to vent. She was shocked but at a loss. That night I went on the air. At 2 a.m., while a Christian program flowed through the speakers, I picked up the phone and woke my Aunt Dee.

I raged. She listened. Then she spoke with a steadiness that cut through the static. "Marvin, this is up to Peggy now. She's fought so hard. Father Regis is human—he's trying to soften the blow. You know if your mom could beat this, she would. Maybe God wants you to know what's coming. You can have hope, but you also must face reality."

After I apologized for the hour and hung up, I fell into a deep well. I had been the strong one, the rock for Dad, the martyr for Mom. Where do you set down fear when you've appointed yourself as the one who carries it all? My aunt had given me a plank across the gap. I suppose, in his way, Father Regis had too.

My mother was dying. I had always known. But if I let go of hope, what remained? How would I look into her eyes tomorrow? Hope was the lifeline that kept the quality of her days intact.

Riverbank Experiences

People told us they were praying. I believed them. After the 2 a.m. call, Aunt Dee came to Maryville for a day. We wandered the hospital corridors, talked in soft circles, and sought counsel from people who knew how to hold holy things without breaking them. One of those voices was Aunt Marilyn.

"Do the kids know your mother is dying?" she asked, sharing how her family had stumbled through a similar transition. I was stunned by the question—and by the answer living inside my silence.

"No," I said finally. "Not really. They know it's serious. We haven't said it out loud."

I didn't realize it then, but Father Regis had tilled the ground so I could plant this hard truth. Dad wasn't up to it. So, I gathered my courage and, when I got home, I called my seven siblings in groups.

First, the older boys: David, Dean, and Norbert. I eased in, but the words still tore. They met the news with resistance, then steadiness—the kind siblings borrow from one another when their world shifts. "We still hope," I said, "but Mama may not make it. She's very sick. She could die."

With my sisters, Linda and Nancy, the words snagged in my throat. Nancy began to giggle—sharp and small at first, then helpless. "It's okay," I told her. "It's a nervous laugh. This is big. You're scared. I am too." She nodded and wiped her eyes, laughing and crying in the same breath.

The hardest were the youngest, Roland and Karl. Karl was in second grade—our open-hearted extrovert, the baby of nine. Roland was quiet, soft-bonded to Mom in a way that made me ache to look at him. They listened carefully and didn't know what to say. I hugged them both and silently begged God for the right words, the right timing, the right mercy.

When the last conversation ended, I sat still and let the relief come. My aunts helped me see what love required. Father Regis had stripped the façade from my denial so I could do the work set before me.

On the drive to Maryville to see Mom, Nancy's voice rose from the back seat. "What is cancer?" she asked. I caught her eyes in the rearview and searched for an answer an eleven-year-old could carry. Somewhere along the line, in holding each other up, Dad and I had failed to keep the kids inside the circle of truth.

The prayers being prayed didn't cure my mother. But they did something—the quiet kind of miracle we only recognize later. They showed me the path for her last days. They gave me courage when I needed courage, words when I needed words, and a strength not my own to walk my brothers and sisters toward goodbye.

And through it all, my mother wore her crucifix—simple, steadfast—testifying with her life to the mystery I was only beginning to see: that love can carry a cross all the way to Calvary and still, somehow, refuse to let despair have the last word.

Reflections and Takeaways

This chapter examines the distinction between clinging and caring: how true hope can coexist with acceptance, and how love tells the truth—even when it hurts.

Hope vs. false hope

- The tension between "believing for a miracle" and "releasing someone to God" is the chapter's central conflict.
- Acceptance isn't surrendering love; it's honoring reality so love can act wisely.

Denial as survival—and its limits

- Silence helped the family cope, but it also delayed crucial conversations (especially with the younger siblings).
- The priest's hard words and the aunts' counsel became the painful catalysts for truth-telling.

Redefining miracles

- The miracle wasn't a cure but time: a summer to celebrate, connect, and say goodbye.
- Ordinary graces—phone calls, visits, the strength to speak hard truths—become sacred.

Agency in illness

- The family doctor's failure to refer to an oncologist raises ethical questions about paternalism and the right to choose one's fight.

- The chapter underscores the need for informed consent, second opinions, and respecting a patient's resolve.

Faith in the fire

- The narrator's faith wavers between protest and trust, revealing how grief exposes what we believe.
- The crucifix Mom wears becomes a living testimony: suffering can be a witness, not a defeat.

Community and intergenerational faith

- Extended family (Aunt Rose, Aunt Dee, Aunt Marilyn) serve as spiritual midwives—translating reality and steadying the heart.
- The grandmother's late baptism and the "lightning bolt" memory highlight how family stories shape belief.

The language of letting go

- "Hand her over to the Lord" lands like a blow yet ultimately opens space for courage and clarity.
- The chapter models how words from spiritual leaders can either wound or wisely prepare—tone and timing matter.

Pivotal moments to carry forward

- Mom's "waterfall" moment: a symbol of peace flowing into pain—an image of passage, cleansing, and presence.
- The two birthdays: joy within sorrow; love insisting on celebration even as time narrows.

- The sibling conversations: love choosing honesty over protection, and discovering that children can hold more truth than we think.

Practical takeaways for readers navigating illness or grief

- Name the reality early, age-appropriately, and often—especially with children.
- Seek second opinions and ensure the patient's voice guides decisions.
- Let community help; invite meaningful visits and conversations.
- Hold two truths at once: hope for what could be, and preparation for what may be.
- Watch for the "small miracles": moments of peace, connection, humor, or sudden courage.

Questions for reflection or discussion

- What does "false hope" look like in my life? What does faithful hope look like?
- When have I mistaken denial for faith—or acceptance for defeat?
- How do I want spiritual leaders to speak to me in crisis—what tone, what timing, what truth?
- What "ordinary miracles" am I overlooking right now?
- If I had to tell hard news to someone younger, how would I do it with honesty and tenderness?

Why this chapter matters

It reframes strength: not as heroic denial, but as the courage to love truthfully. It shows that faith doesn't erase grief; it accompanies the transformation of the final stretch of a life into a witness to love, dignity, and quiet grace.

CHAPTER THIRTEEN
The Aftermath

"Fear not, for I am with you; be not dismayed, for I am your God; I will strengthen you, I will help you, I will uphold you with my righteous right hand."

Isaiah 41:10

My mother was fading fast. She no longer ate, yet every knock at her hospital door revived something bright in her eyes. Women I'd never met came in waves, their voices soft and eager, carrying stories of a blond-curled girl who once turned corridors into runways and classrooms into stages. Their memories felt like sunlight in a room that had grown dim.

At the center of those weeks stood Teddy Runde—my mother's "sister," bound not by blood but by the Kansas City Diocese catechism program. They were opposites in so many ways and yet inseparable in the only way that counted. As Karl and Roland settled into school and the older kids learned to babysit, Mom's world widened. God called her beyond our house, and she answered with both feet and her whole heart.

"You know we're all praying for Peggy," Teddy said when I walked in one afternoon. She clasped my hand and held it, her eyes shining. "I couldn't have asked for a better sister."

I looked at Mom and finally understood—their vow wasn't spoken, it was lived. They were sisters in Christ.

Stumbling into regrets

Linda turned thirteen on Tuesday, October 16. We refused to let the day shrink under the weight of illness. The party came to Mom. We laughed, told stories, and showed her the cake she couldn't eat. She leaned into the music of the room, and for an hour, we forgot.

The next day, I came back, still warm from the celebration's glow. Mom sat up, cheeks lit with a rare color. "When are we celebrating Linda's birthday?" she asked, almost playful. "I'm feeling rather chipper today."

I stopped. Then I stumbled. "Mom—it was yesterday. Don't you remember?"

The joy in her face collapsed. She folded into herself, as if something heavy had struck her from within, and a day had gone by. A day she couldn't hold. I took her hand and pushed past the elephant standing at the foot of the bed. "We'll make the most of what we have," I whispered, unsure who I was trying to convince.

Thursday evening, the phone at her bedside rang. I answered brightly, "Hello."

"Yeah, Marvin, we're getting ready to come over," David said.

"Sure thing, David," I began—but Mom shook her head, slowly, firmly. Eyes closed. Dad held her hand, uncertain, helpless.

"Ah, David," I said, the words catching on my tongue, "maybe you better not come over tonight. Mom's not feeling up to it. Maybe tomorrow."

It was the last chance any of us would have to see her alive. I let her decide. Years later, I'd understand the fragile math of grief: the tug-of-war between honoring a request and protecting a regret. David learned only much later that I had been the messenger, not the author.

Counting to Three

On Friday afternoon, October 19, 1984, I called the radio station to say I wouldn't be in for my weekend shifts. Denial had been my armor for weeks. It fell off without a sound.

"There was a second death on the floor last night," Dad said. His voice was steady, reverent. "Things happen in threes. I've seen it before." He wasn't predicting. He was preparing.

Grandma Naomi and Grandpa Roy were exhausted from the vigil. Dad convinced them to go home and rest. Grandma's own grief trailed her like a long shadow—she had missed her father's last breath and had never forgiven herself. Now she needed to step back before her body betrayed her heart.

Aunt Donna drove to the farmhouse after school, made supper for the younger kids, and shepherded the four youngest to my brother Vincent's. The three boys stayed with Grandma and Grandpa Tuttle. I, too, reached my limit. As Mom's breathing grew shallow and the nurses grew tender, I went to my brother's house to sleep. Dad stayed. My brother stayed. And Grandma Gertrude sat beside my mother, thumbing her rosary, prayer by steady prayer.

Dreams in the night

Not long after I drifted off to sleep, a burst of pure light filled my dream. No faces. No words. Just radiance—and peace so complete it felt like gravity had changed its mind.

I opened my eyes. My brother stood in the doorway. He didn't have to speak.

My mother had died.

At St. Joseph's, the women prayed without ceasing for their sister Peggy. They had cooked with her, worked bazaars with her, laughed and grieved beside her. Their parish had already known loss—Orville Durbin, then David Runde. Now Peggy lay in a bed at St. Francis.

That night, after supper and television, Pat Auffert drifted off with Peggy in her prayers. The phone rang—clear as a bell in a dream.

"Hello," Pat said, rubbing sleep from her eyes.

"Pat, I just wanted to thank you for all you and the church have done for my family and me. I love you."

"Love you too."

She jolted upright into darkness. It was a dream—but it wasn't nothing. She cried. She knew. And when morning came, she promised she'd pass the message on.

Safely Home

The next twelve hours blurred. Dad, my brother, and I drove to Ravenwood to tell Grandma and Grandpa. David, Dean, and Norbert were staying there, too. On the way, we stopped for Grandma's brother, Victor, and his wife, Thelma, so my grandparents wouldn't have to stand in the first wave alone.

"Oh my God," Grandpa said, the words breaking open. "If only she had seen her kids graduate. Why couldn't she see her kids graduate?"

I rubbed his back, feeling his frame quake. Grandma broke down in tears. "My little girl," Naomi wept as Victor steadied her.

Plans rose out of our shock like scaffolding—dates, music, readings. We set up the service quickly. None of us realized until the day arrived that Dean's sixteenth birthday was caught in the undertow.

Rosaries and Realizations

At the family rosary, relatives filed past us with hands and hugs and words that barely held themselves together. Karl's grief poured out of him unfiltered; Roland sat quiet as stone. Each of us grieved in our own language.

On Sunday night, after the parish rosary, a family friend embraced me without warning. "Thank you for all you did for her," he whispered, eyes wet.

For the first time, the year gathered itself in my chest. I had pressed pause on my life. I hadn't owned it; I had given it—willingly, entirely. It felt like a kind of martyrdom, and it would shape everything that came after. I didn't deliberate. I just did what love required.

Later, while I shook hands and murmured "thank you" to line after line of faces, I slipped back to a small living room in Hobbs, New Mexico, to a prayer I'd once whispered. Yesterday was gone, tomorrow unrevealed, and grief's cold fingers curled around my throat. Who was I now, if not the advocate, the caregiver, my father's confidant?

The Funeral: Song, Cross, and Sunlight

The church was full. In the casket, Mom looked impossibly small. The peace on her face startled me for the joy it stirred. She was done with pain; that much was certain. The music rose—Amazing Grace and How Great Thou Art—and the floor might as well have trembled. I sang with a voice I didn't know I had. Dad's voice was loudest. She was safely home.

At the end, Father Regis pressed something into Dad's hand, tears too near to hide. We walked into the sunlight, stood together as pallbearers guided the casket to the hearse. Dad opened his palm. There lay a crucifix—like the one Mom had worn through her illness, the one he made sure was pinned to her dress in preparation for her burial. Another cross for our road.

We didn't need words. We had reached the mountaintop of our father-and-son life, and for once, silence said everything. Mom's cancer had been her cross. Now we would shoulder ours.

The Final Goodbye

At the cemetery, people spoke in hushed voices, as if volume might disturb the ground that would soon hold her. When the casket lowered, the weight settled on us that no one person could lift.

An elderly woman from the parish wrapped me in a fierce hug. "If you think this is bad, just wait," she said. I blinked, stunned. What kind of thing do you say to the grieving?

It sounded like doom, but those words outlasted the day. In time, I realized her sentence was a message, not a malediction. Not a prophecy of despair but a nod to "the process"—the long work of grief and the stubborn flame of hope.

Father Regis had preached, "He will do greater things." Years earlier, after a broken engagement, Scripture had taught me, "All things work together for the good." At the Parnell Cemetery, between the whisper of grass and the ache of dirt, I was asked to let go—again. A week earlier, Father Regis had urged me to release her into God's hands. I wasn't ready. Maybe it wasn't meant to be until now..

The line between redeeming hope and false hope is as thin as breath. Late on Friday, October 19, Mom waited until the room was quiet—until we were gone or praying—to slip free. She knew the difference.

If you think this is bad, just wait.

Maybe she was right. Maybe life would ask for more. But what I carried wasn't false hope; it was faith. Today my hope was simple: Mom was no longer suffering. We were.

Happiness, I've learned, is found along the way, not at the end of the road. What is it that everyone is searching for? Mom had seen it. In a short time, she touched many lives. And when given two months to live, she turned it into nine—a long goodbye calibrated by grace. She refused the poison of bitterness.

In all joy, there is sadness; in all sadness, there is joy.

A year earlier, I wouldn't have understood that. After that woman's words faded, joy did the strangest thing—it returned. I knew the bright light that filled my dream was my mother's parting gift, a final kiss of radiance. God let us say goodbye in the only language that never falters.

Light.

Reflections and Takeaways

This chapter sits in the tender space between holding on and letting go. It portrays grief not as a single event but as a series of thresholds—birthdays at bedsides, last-minute decisions, a bright dream at the exact hour of passing, a crucifix pressed into a palm. Community becomes both balm and mirror: parish women praying, family gathering, a priest weeping, an elderly woman's hard word that later turns into wisdom.

The narrator realizes that love can look like sacrifice—"a form of martyrdom"—and that hope, when purified by faith, is not denial but the courage to accept what is. The story honors the sacredness of ordinary acts (cake delivered to a hospital room, a rosary whispered through the night) and shows how symbols—light, the cross, a phone call that arrives in a dream—carry us across the valley when language fails.

Core Themes and Symbols

- Sisters in Christ: Spiritual kinship (Teddy and Peggy) as real family.
- Thresholds of time: A birthday celebrated twice—once in presence, once forgotten—reveals the fragility of memory and the persistence of love.
- Agency vs. regret: The choice to honor a loved one's wishes (declining a visit) becomes a lifelong teacher.
- Communal grief: Rosaries, casseroles, and crowded pews—ritual as a container for sorrow.

- Liminal experiences: A radiant dream and a friend's "phone call" in sleep as consolations at the boundary of life and death.
- The Cross as motif: A crucifix passed from priest to father signifies a shared calling to carry on.
- "If you think this is bad, just wait": Initially jarring, later reframed as a truth about the process of grief and the endurance of hope.

Life Takeaways

- Both/and is holy: Joy and sorrow can coexist; relief and ache are not contradictions.
- Honor your wishes; name the trade-offs: Loving choices may carry later regret—speak openly, document your intent, and forgive yourself.
- Rituals matter: Prayers, songs, and gatherings give shape to the formlessness of loss.
- Mark milestones even in crisis: Celebrations at the bedside create anchors for memory.
- Symbols sustain: Objects (a crucifix), and moments (a dream of light) can become lasting sources of strength.
- Community holds what we can't: Let others pray, cook, drive, sit—receive as much as you give.
- Hope vs. false hope: Faith doesn't deny death; it faces it with trust and tenderness.

Faith and Meaning

- Surrender is not defeat: Releasing a loved one into God's hands is an act of love, not abandonment.
- Consolations come strangely: Dreams, "coincidences," and unexpected words can carry divine comfort.
- The cross continues: After a loved one's suffering ends, those who remain are invited to carry forward love's work.

Discussion/Reflection Questions

- When should we honor a loved one's wishes even if it risks future regret?
- How do you interpret "liminal" experiences (dreams, signs) in grief?
- Where is the line between hope and denial in your own life?
- What personal "cross" are you being asked to carry forward?

In this chapter, a family learns to let go through faith, ritual, and the quiet language of symbols—discovering that love's last lesson is not how to hold on, but how to carry on.

CHAPTER FOURTEEN

Ashes to Ashes, Dust to Dust

"...So that the proof of your faith, being more precious than gold, which is perishable, even though tested by fire, may be found to result in praise and glory and honor at the revelation of Jesus Christ..."

1 PETER: 1: 7

The weeks after Mom died didn't pass so much as they settled—like frost creeping down the window, inch by inch, until the view disappears. November hollowed the house. The phone went quiet. Neighbors and cousins who once checked in drifted back to their lives, while we were asked, gently and then not-so-gently, to get on with ours.

At school, my younger brothers and sisters were no longer wrapped in extra patience. The message came in small, practical ways: make up the homework, get to class on time, stop crying. As if grief were a switch you could flip when the bell rang.

Karl, my youngest brother, would be eight in a week. He wore worries like a jacket no one could see. One evening, he stood square in front of me while Dad and I argued with the evening news about the state of the world.

"My birthday is next week," he announced.

"Yes, and you'll be eight. That's exciting," I said.

He held my gaze steady as a fencepost in a winter field.

"What's on your mind?" I asked.

"I don't have anyone to take birthday treats to my class."

His voice was calm, almost polite, as if he were asking for another napkin instead of a normal life. My laugh came out thin and nervous—because I knew exactly what he was asking, and who would have to become what Mom had been.

"Oh, well, you can have a birthday party at school."

And just like that, my name was on the assignment. The second-grade room looked the same as when Mrs. Lewis had scolded me for "teaching her class." But this time, I came bearing cupcakes and a brother who grinned like sunrise. For a day, the world fit back into place for him, and I let myself breathe.

As Christmas lights went up around town, the air in our house turned heavy. The silence had a sound to it—the space where Mom's voice should have been. It slipped into the bedroom and down the hallway, and Dad and I would catch each other looking at the door as if she might call out any second. Even my grandparents—the steady, stoic types—were losing their footing. When we drove over to see them one cold afternoon, their smiles were slower to arrive. Grief rearranges the furniture and then swears nothing's changed. Depression followed close behind.

Questions linger

Mom's social club invited our family to their December meeting. I said yes and then spent the morning wondering where exactly I belonged in the world. I hadn't exactly been job-hunting; I'd been filling the gaps Mom left behind and letting the clock run over me. Dad and I became each other's ballast. President Reagan was elected to his second term, the headlines rolled past, and our little world kept holding its breath.

Aunt Dee came over with my sister-in-law, Joan, to do the unthinkable: go through Mom's clothes. We decided to do it while Dad was in the field. We wanted to protect him from the moment of it—from the scent of her perfume rising out of sweaters, from the weight of her blouses in our hands.

But grief has a nose for secrets.

"Why is everyone walking on eggshells around me?" Dad demanded later, face flushed, eyes bright with hurt and anger and something deeper neither of us could name.

I didn't have a good answer. None of us did. We wanted to spare each other the pain, as if pain could be spared. It seeped through anyway, finding us where we were most breakable.

Questions found me, too. At Mass, Father Regis sharpened his sermons into something that felt like a direct address. Words about service and calling and surrender seemed to lift off the ambo and hover over my pew. Maybe the priest who'd helped me through my broken engagement had been right. Maybe God was calling me to something I hadn't planned.

"That is a big, big decision," Aunt Dee said, the three of us parked around the table, delaying the closet, delaying everything.

"You've just been through a major trauma. You need to really pray about that."

She was right, as usual. I could feel God using her voice to steady my own. I did what she told me: I handed the question over. If this was the path, I asked God to show me. If it wasn't, I asked Him to close the door.

Door of opportunity

Two years earlier, in 1982, Mom and Dad had driven me across three states with a stack of résumés and an aircheck box packed in the backseat. Trenton, Missouri. Red Oak, Iowa. Atchison, Kansas. We turned in tapes, shook hands, laughed our way through diner pies, and called it a valiant try. Then life shifted. I went to two other stations. 1984 arrived like a storm front.

On a sharp December afternoon, the kitchen phone rang. I expected an aunt to check in or a neighbor with church news.

"I remember you visited our radio station a while back and dropped off an aircheck and résumé," the voice said. "I wondered if you were still interested in a position with our station."

KARE Radio was based in Atchison, Kansas which was an hour and a half from the farm.

That tape had collected two years of dust. My life had collected a decade's worth of upheaval. Still, there it was: a door I hadn't knocked on in months swinging open. I set the interview. That evening, we would go to Mom's club's Christmas dinner; after, I'd drive to Shenandoah for my Friday night shift. The timing felt like a wink from heaven. Maybe the answer to my prayer wasn't a collar. Maybe it was a microphone.

Maybe joy would come in the morning. Maybe the horizon was clearing.

The fiery furnace

I drove home at dawn from my overnight shift, singing to the radio, drumming my fingers on the steering wheel. The hill above the farmhouse lifted me high enough to see the yard, and my heart stuttered at the sight of Dad's pickup backed up crooked to the porch.

He never parked like that.

I followed the prickling at the back of my neck up the steps. Dad met me at the door, a grin too big and too bright across his face.

"We had an interesting night," he said, taking off his hat and rubbing his head in the same manner the young man from my childhood did when he announced it was time for a change. "When we got home, we discovered the kitchen was on fire."

The smell hit me when I stepped inside—thick, bitter smoke layered over everything we owned. The walls wore gray stains like a tide line. Dad walked me through it. Flames had been low and mean, throwing orange light against the kitchen windows when they pulled in. He sent the older boys to the neighbors to call 911 and kept the younger kids in the truck while he went in, crawling, face near the floor, hands searching for heat—because the smoke sealed the air off at chest height.

The kitchen floor had been a shallow lake of fire. He knew right away he couldn't fight it—too much smoke, too hungry a flame. He backed out before the house could pull the fire deeper into its lungs. Volunteer trucks crowded the drive and the yard, lights stuttering against the trees. They got it out. They saved the house.

The culprit was almost laughable in the daylight: a defective coffee pot plug. The pot had been switched off. It didn't matter. Fire had its own ideas.

We walked the wreckage together. The barometer on the wall hung in a melted slump, a brass clock-face turned to candlewax. Above it, my parents' thirtieth anniversary portrait stared back at me untouched—no soot, no singe, as if the glass itself had drawn a boundary.

A miracle, I thought. She's watching.

How else to explain a fire that didn't run the rafters, a barometer that melted from the heat while the picture above it did not? How else to explain that every one of us had been out of the house when the cord sparked alive?

I didn't sleep between shifts that day. We opened windows. We told the story back and forth until it cracked, and then we laughed in the way people laughed when the alternative is breaking apart.

"So, what else can there be?" I muttered, half-joking, remembering the flood that had turned my Hobbs, New Mexico, place into a shallow lake earlier that year.

This made three: the flood, Linda's fever—104 degrees, the quiet drive to the Maryville ER—and now the fire. Dad took me through each room, shaking his head.

"There's nothing to do but dig in and put things back together," he said. "We were fortunate the whole house didn't go up in flames. Most of the smoke damage is upstairs. Everything is covered in smoke."

The getting-back-to-work began before the last hose rolled up. My uncles—Raymond and Joe—showed up with their wives, my brother Vincent and his, and by noon the yard looked like a moving day gone wrong. We saved what we could, hauled blackened furniture to the machine shed, and said goodbye to what couldn't be salvaged. My album collection—years of soundtracks—curled into crackling ruin. It felt like pieces of the past went up in smoke even as other parts of it, painful and precious both, returned to haunt the air.

We laundered. We scrubbed walls until our shoulders screamed. We planned. When the insurance adjuster finished his sifting and the report came back mostly merciful, Dad exhaled a long breath and took a shopping list to town.

For a while, our family scattered again: Linda, Nancy, Roland, and Karl to my grandparents in Ravenwood; David, Dean, and Norbert to Joe and Donna's. Dad and I bunked there too, tripping over kindness and borrowed blankets.

Word got out—small towns are good at that—and a reporter from the St. Joseph Gazette came to walk the rooms with us. The story ran with just the right tilt: tragedy threaded with something inexplicable and kind. I said what felt true, because it was the only thing holding us all up: faith had carried us through Mom's death and now through this.

A few days later, the KARE program manager called back. He'd read the piece before my interview, he said later. When I'd sat down across from him, I felt a steadiness I hadn't felt in months, like the chair had four legs and the floor wasn't moving.

The offer came that week.

Everyone cheered—Dad, Aunt Donna and Uncle Joe, my brother and sister-in-law, cousins who'd been running casseroles and clean laundry out to the farm. It was time, they said. Time to let 1984 loosen its grip on us. Time for me to step toward my own life again.

After everything—the sermons, the prayers at the kitchen table, the door I'd asked God to close or open—the question of the priesthood melted back into the grain of the smoke-stained wood and disappeared. The call had been real; the answer was, too. It just happened to come through a microphone instead of a pulpit.

And when I packed my car to drive toward Atchison, the picture from the kitchen drifted through my mind: the barometer warped into silence, the anniversary portrait gleaming clean above it.

Loss and mercy stacked one atop the other: fire and the future.

I confidently turned the key and the morning opened.

Reflections and Takeaways

This chapter traces a powerful arc from numbing grief to fragile hope, using ordinary moments—a child's birthday, a closet of clothes, a faulty coffee plug—to ask what holds a family together when the center is gone. It's a chapter about vocation (in every sense), survival, and the surprising ways grace can arrive.

What the chapter is "about" (beneath the plot)

- Grief's quiet persistence: The silence after Mom's death becomes a character—thick, unavoidable, shaping every decision.
- Responsibility re-shuffled: Adult roles shift fast; a sibling steps in for a mother so a second grader can still have cupcakes.
- Discernment in the dark: The narrator wrestles with a calling (priesthood vs. radio), learning that clarity often comes through circumstances, not just contemplation.
- Crisis as catalyst: A literal fire refines priorities, tests community bonds, and strangely clears a path forward.
- Faith in the ordinary: "Miracles" appear not as spectacle but as timing, preservation, and protection (an untouched anniversary photo; a providential phone call).

Key themes and insights

- Nonlinear grief: Compassion from others fades while grief remains—especially for children navigating "normal" expectations.

- The language of need in children: Karl's calm request reveals how kids ask for stability without drama.
- The tender politics of grief: Clearing a closet can be both healing and wounding; attempts to "protect" each other often backfire.
- Calling vs. circumstance: The sermons awaken a question; the job offer answers it—different altar, same service.
- Providence and protection: The coffee pot plug causes chaos; the family's absence and the preserved photo hint at mercy within loss.
- Community as scaffolding: Extended family, neighbors, the parish, and even a newspaper knit a safety net.

Symbols and motifs

- Winter/quiet: Emotional hibernation; a home that feels airless without a voice.
- Birthday treats: A child-size ritual of normalcy, asserting continuity amid rupture.
- The closet: A threshold between memory and forward motion; touching fabric becomes touching grief.
- The pickup backed to the porch: A visual alarm—something is off—ushering in the fire scene.
- Barometer vs. photo: Time and weather "melt," but covenant/endurance remains untouched.
- Door/phone call: Vocation reframed less about escaping pain, more about stepping into giftedness.

Character dynamics

- Narrator and Dad: A partnership built on mutual ballast—love expressed through logistics, labor, and dark humor.
- Karl: His steadiness calls the family to continue simple joys; he anchors "what must not be lost."
- Aunt Dee: A spiritual compass who slows rash decisions; wisdom with warmth.
- Father Regis: A catalytic voice prompting honest discernment.
- The wider family: A working chorus—scrub brushes, machine shed triage, casseroles, practical grace.

Key takeaways

- Grief doesn't respect clocks or calendars; institutions do. That gap creates friction.
- Small acts of normalcy (cupcakes, shared chores) are lifelines.
- Protecting each other from pain can isolate; honest participation in loss is kinder.
- Discernment often emerges through "doors" that open (or don't) rather than pure introspection.
- Crisis concentrates community; restoration is communal, not solitary.
- Faith often manifests as timing, protection, and enough provision for the next step.

Reflection questions for readers/journaling

- Where have you mistaken silence for healing—or busyness for recovery?

- What "cupcake-sized" act could restore a sense of normalcy for someone grieving?
- Have you ever cleared a loved one's belongings? What did that reveal about your grief?
- Which doors are opening in your life that might be answers to older prayers?
- What's your "untouched photo"—something preserved against the odds that reminds you you're held?

Life applications

- Build rituals of continuity after loss (birthdays, seasonal traditions) to stabilize children.
- Communicate openly about grief tasks (like sorting belongings) to avoid unintended hurt.
- Practice "discernment by reality": notice opportunities, timing, and energy rather than waiting for perfect certainty.
- Lean into community help; let people carry different pieces of the burden.
- Look for signs of mercy in the margins of crisis; name them aloud.

This chapter doesn't claim that pain is erased; it shows how, within the scorch marks, a future can still take shape. Vocation, in the end, is less about escaping sorrow and more about offering your voice—into the silence that grief leaves behind.

PART THREE

DESTINY ARRIVES

Rollin' at sea, adrift on the water,
could it be finally I'm turnin' for home?
Finally a chance to say, "Hey, I love you"
Never again to be all alone.

'Cause you light up my life,
You give me hope to carry on,
You light up my days and fill my nights with song,

DEBBY BOONE, YOU LIGHT UP MY LIFE

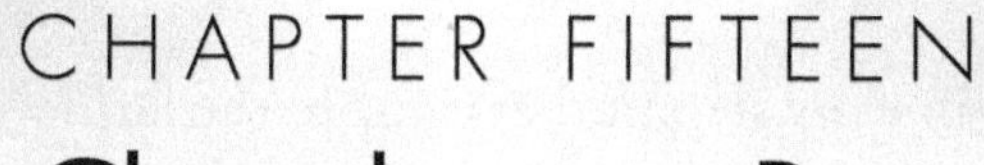

CHAPTER FIFTEEN
Cherokee or Bust

"Happiness is letting go of what you think your life is supposed to look like and celebrating it for everything that it is."

Mandy Hale

"Trust in the LORD with all your heart, and do not lean on your own understanding. In all your ways acknowledge him, and he will make straight your paths."

Proverbs 3: 5

I walked away from radio in early 1986 without a plan—only a pulse. The year behind me had frayed the edges of who I thought I was: my moods swung like a door in a storm, and reality felt a half-step out of rhythm. I wouldn't understand that year for decades. But turning my back on the booth and the board was the first clean choice I'd made in a long time.

The trouble didn't start at work. It started at home.

In November 1985, a year after Mom died, Dad remarried. I stood beside him as best man, a role I never applied for and didn't know how to play. Months earlier, at a cousin's wedding, he'd announced the engagement from upstairs near the cake table, then tugged me aside downstairs and asked me to stand with him. I said yes because that's what a loyal son does. But grief and gratitude are uneasy neighbors, and that year they fought over every square inch inside me.

The first time my stepmother came to the farm was for David's graduation. My brother sat in his cap and gown, and a new woman sat beside our father. We were still figuring out where to put our hands, our eyes, our loyalty. I told myself I was fine. I told myself a lot of things.

Anger found an easier target than the man in Dad's chair. I picked fights at KARE Radio, I didn't have to choose. I called it "creative differences." It was grief—raw, wandering, and loud. Better the boss than my father. Better the job than the family.

When I finally left my radio days at the start of 1986, I drifted through a call center for six months, ears ringing with other people's problems. Then I shook myself awake and walked into The Maryville Daily Forum. During the tour, they gave me a trial assignment; I wrote it cleanly and quickly. The newsroom was small and hungry, exactly my kind of church.

I learned the rhythm. Features by day. City council and school board by night. Friday marathons that ran from a PM edition into a Saturday morning paper as if time were a rubber band. Sixty hours a week, and it didn't feel like work. I developed a shorthand that resembled lightning strikes and translated it into copy that sang. My farm upbringing had trained my hands to move, my military service trained my mind to watch, and the newsroom trained my heart to listen.

Every morning, Grandma Tuttle unfolded the paper and found my byline with a reverence that humbled me. "Peggy's boy," her friends said, with that sigh people save for the dead and the accomplished. I carried her pride like a medal I hadn't earned yet.

And still, restlessness itched under my skin.

By late summer 1987, I met Kathy. She was bright, warm, a second chance at something I kept telling myself I didn't need. We went on a date while I stared down a crossroads. I had answered a help-wanted ad in Cherokee, Iowa, two hundred miles north and, if I was honest, a galaxy away from the life that had settled around me in Maryville.

I had been a rolling stone since 1980, when a broken engagement left a long, thin scar I didn't like to touch. Two years later came June, the sweetest kind of summer romance. She had a job waiting in Fort Madison. I had a stack of rejections and a Catholic faith that didn't match her Methodist roots. We didn't fight about it; the distance did the arguing for us. When I reached out from Hobbs, New Mexico, I learned she'd gone back to an old boyfriend. Ghosts travel light; they're good at finding you.

When the editor in Cherokee called and invited me to an interview, I said yes before my doubts arose. I drove four hours on a Saturday, fed coins into the box out front, bought the paper I hoped one day would pay me to write, and felt something in me align. The editor drove me around town—past the high school, downtown, a quiet stretch of trees—and then swung by the Cherokee Mental Health Institute.

"A lot of folks don't even know this is here," he said.

I did the math fast and wrong. Kathy was studying psychology. Maybe she could move up, too. Maybe there was a world where careers and love rode in the same car and never argued over the radio.

I called her. We went out one more time. I painted the picture: the job, the town, the institute. She listened kindly, then tilted the painting back toward me. "There's a reason for everything," she said, and told me to forget about her and go.

I was tired of moving on, but not moving at all scared me more.

A week later, I took a call at my desk in Maryville as I was packing for the night. "It's Cherokee," a coworker said, breathless at my door. I ran back to the phone like a kid to a bell.

"Marvin," the editor said, "our publisher approved it. We'd like to offer you the position."

I said yes before the sentence finished. Then I drove straight to the farm, my heart racing ahead of the car. In the living room, I took my old spot at the end of the couch. Dad settled into his chair; my stepmother into hers. One of my sisters handed me a celebratory cup of coffee. I told them everything—the town, the paper, the pages I could already see my name on. I waited for Dad's smile.

He ran a hand through his hair, the way he did when I was a boy and he was breaking free from his own father. "I'm concerned," he said at last. "It seems you're always going off on some tangent and changing jobs. You've got a good job now."

I don't remember my exact words, only that they came out hot and true. That if I didn't claim my life now, I never would. That this wasn't a tangent—it was a road.

Later, I called Grandma. Her joy surprised me. She was a homebody by nature and by heart, but she saw what Cherokee could mean. She'd watched my name climb to the front page day after day;

now, she imagined it traveling. She quietly clipped all my stories and pasted them into a scrapbook.

She spoke of me with pride until I believed it.

I'd told God for years that if He opened a door, I'd walk through it, even if my hands shook on the knob. Cherokee felt less like an exit and more like an answer. There was tension brewing in the family, an unrest I couldn't fix by standing still. Maybe God wanted me out of the blast zone long enough to work on me alone. Maybe He was readying me for the promises I kept hearing about but couldn't hold yet—work that mattered, love that stayed.

Dad would have to learn to let go. So, would I.

I packed boxes. I made lists. I said goodbye. And then I turned north, toward a small-town newsroom where my creative juices flowed like honey, patient and sure.

Reflections and Takeaways

This chapter chronicles a pivotal identity shift: from grief-worn son and restless worker to self-claiming writer following a call to Cherokee, Iowa.

It interweaves family upheaval (father's remarriage), vocational discovery (newspapering), and complicated love—filtered through faith and a growing sense of destiny.

Core themes

- Grief's disguise: Anger at a boss masks unspoken grief toward a father and the loss of "the old family."
- Vocation as salvation: Journalism becomes both craft and container—transmuting pain into purpose.
- Individuation: The "barnburner" speech marks a boundary with Dad—an adult claim to one's own path.
- Patterns and ghosts: Repeating relational hesitations (1979–80 engagement, 1982 June, 1987 Kathy) reveal a fear of attachment and the need to let go.
- Faith and providence: Open doors, "calls," and timing suggest a theology of movement—God's guidance through transition.
- Belonging vs. becoming: Hometown roots and family expectations press against the pull of growth and risk.

Key turning points

- 1985: Dad's remarriage; narrator as best man—duty colliding with grief.

- Early 1986: Leaving radio—rage redirected from family to workplace.
- Mid–late 1986: Discovery of newspaper work—flow, stamina, and validation (Grandma's proud ritual of reading the byline).
- 1987: The Cherokee interview and offer—an external yes matching an internal call.
- The living-room scene: Waiting for Dad's approval, receiving caution instead; choosing self-determination.
- Final assent: Saying yes to Cherokee despite relational uncertainty with Kathy.

Character arc

- From: Reactive, displaced anger, approval-seeking son.
- Through: Hard-won competence, daily discipline, and honest self-observation.
- To: A more self-directed adult with boundaries, purpose, and a faith-anchored courage to move.

Symbolic moments

- The newspaper box coins: Investing in a future self before it's certain.
- Dad's hand through hair: Echo of his own earlier break from his father—history repeating, then evolving.
- The byline: Tangible identity and a legacy thread connecting the narrator, his mother, and Grandma.

- The chairs in the living room: A new family order—absence and replacement rendered in space.
- The press's thunder: The soundscape of becoming—work as heartbeat.

What the chapter says about work

- Passion fuels endurance, but the grind is real: 60-hour weeks, PM-to-morning turnarounds.
- Competence becomes a stabilizer—shorthand to prose, observation to insight.
- Community journalism offers purpose: being the eyes and ears, fighting for the underdog, telling both sides.

What the chapter says about love

- Patterns of hesitation and mistrust linger from earlier wounds.
- "Quick math" fantasies (Kathy + Cherokee MHI) show a longing to align vocation and intimacy—before trust is established.
- Letting go is painful but clarifying; sometimes the career step must precede relational wholeness.

Destiny and Faith throughlines

- Discernment by doors: when they open, step.
- Removal from "the blast zone": distance as divine strategy for growth.
- Promise-in-process: Work that matters now; love that may follow later.

Key takeaways

- Grief often hides behind anger; address the root, not just the reaction.
- Purposeful work can alchemize pain—and reveal true vocation.
- Differentiation from parents is a necessary, sometimes painful rite of passage.
- Repeating relational patterns signal unresolved fear; awareness is the first pivot.
- Restlessness can be a compass—listen when it points toward growth.
- External validation (Grandma's pride) can counter internal doubt—receive it, but don't depend on it.
- Faith-informed risk-taking means saying yes before certainty arrives.
- Boundaries create room for calling—and for healthier love later.

Questions for reflection

- Where are you displacing anger that belongs to a more profound grief?
- What work makes time disappear—and what does that reveal about calling?
- Which family scripts are you still obeying, and which must you rewrite?

- What "quick math" fantasies do you use to avoid more challenging conversations?
- Which open door in your life deserves a yes, even if your hands shake?

A son steps out of grief's shadow, claims his vocation, and chooses the uncertain road to become the person his work—and his faith—are calling him to be.

CHAPTER SIXTEEN
Cue Lines, Headlines, and Grace

"We never know how God will answer our prayers, but we can expect that He will get us involved in His plan for the answer. If we are true intercessors, we must be ready to take part in God's work on behalf of the people for whom we pray."

Corrie ten Boom

"Ask, and it will be given to you; seek, and you will find; knock, and it will be opened to you. For everyone who asks receives, and he who seeks finds, and to him who knocks it will be opened. Or what man is there among you who, when his son asks for a loaf will give him a stone? Or if he asks for a fish, he will not give him a snake, will he? If you then, being evil, know how to give good gifts to your children, how much more will your Father who is in heaven give what is good to those who ask Him!"

Matthew 7: 7-11

I arrived in Cherokee with most of my life in the backseat and a prayer in my chest. I'd drifted into other towns before, but Cherokee felt different—less like a stopover and more like a gentle hand at my back. I didn't so much choose Cherokee as it chose me. Maybe God did the choosing.

The Cherokee Daily Times ran Tuesday through Saturday. The town still nursed a grudge about losing Monday's paper, but the new rhythm suited my soul. Evenings in the newsroom replaced frantic afternoons; Friday night scores made Saturday's edition. My sixty-hour marathons shrank to something more human, and the day broke into small, livable shifts. I found a kind of Sabbath rest in better pacing.

I did what I knew to do—show up, listen hard, write fair. Budget hearings turned into spiritual practice: stand in the tension, tell the truth, don't take sides that don't belong to you. Between the County Board of Supervisors and the Taxpayers Association, I wrote with both sets of shoes on. Respect came not as applause but as quiet nods—the kind of affirmation that feels like God's whisper: Keep going.

The 1988 Iowa caucuses brought every candidate to our corner of the state. Gymnasiums and cafeterias filled like revival tents of democracy. I covered them all. Vice President Bush packed Washington High School, the choreography of security threading through small-town wonder. He'd win the White House, but in Iowa he finished behind Dole and Robertson—a reminder that crowns are lent, not owned, and momentum is God's to give or withhold. I lived for the unscripted moments when a candidate's eyes went off-teleprompter and told the truth.

Rebounds, Laments, and Letting Go

Work was a vocation now, but my heart lagged, still bandaging old wounds. I wrote to Kathy one more time—my last try at resurrecting something God had already buried. Her reply was kind and final. I whispered "good riddance" like a small exorcism and dropped the letter in the trash.

Then came Rhonda—tall, careful, newly divorced, not seeking. We offered each other companionship more than romance, a layover more than a destination. When her guard dropped, we laughed. Mostly, the drawbridge stayed up. I released it. Letting go is also a form of prayer.

Restlessness circled again—job postings, the itch to move. My father's old line echoed: Would this rolling stone ever stop rolling? I asked God the same question and tried to listen.

Providence in a Doorway

An editor role in Atlantic called to my ambition. I interviewed. Then my publisher paused in a doorway and altered my map: a raise and the title of assistant editor—offered on the spot. It felt like providence arriving without fanfare.

I said yes. Minutes later, Atlantic called with an offer of their own. For the first time, I said no. The word felt like I'd stepped into a room God had been preparing while I wore myself out knocking on other doors. A dial turned inside me without my effort. Nights at the press, more responsibility, more money—less wanderlust. The foundation is poured and setting.

A Stage, A Script, A Calling

With my first paid vacation ahead—my brother David's wedding pulling me back to Missouri—I knew I needed to root deeper in Cherokee. The community theatre announced auditions. I asked my editor for coverage if I landed a part. "Sure," she said, smiling. Ruby, our silver-haired Lifestyles sage, chuckled: "He just wants to meet some cute young thing." Maybe. Mostly, I wanted to breathe different air.

The play was Alone Together. Michael—the lead—was thirty and moving back in with his parents. The script read like a mirror I wasn't sure I wanted to peer into. The third-act father-son clash felt uncomfortably familiar. If acting is prayer with your whole body, I knew I could pray this one honestly.

At auditions, a quiet young woman said she preferred backstage work. "Lori," she introduced herself—Lori Chihak. The name slipped past me for the moment. I got the role, tucked the playbook beside my suit for the wedding, and drove home.

Missouri had shifted. Without my mother's center of gravity, the farm felt like a beloved house after the furniture's been moved. My father was newly married; my siblings older in ways I couldn't measure. I loved them, and I missed what we had been. Gratitude made room for both truths.

Driving back to Cherokee in the dark, the sky opened. A shooting star tore across the night—bright, startling, unmistakable. I received it the way you receive a benediction you didn't know you were waiting for. I felt, deeply, that the past had released me, and God had turned the page.

Cue Lines and Quiet Leadings

Back at rehearsal, my stage parents needed help with lines. The director called in a prompter: Lori. I noticed her—then noticed I wasn't trying to. Opening weekend arrived, and the audience's laughter rose like a warm tide. Theatre is communal breath; I felt carried.

Saturday, Lori didn't show. Sunday matinee, she returned and giggled that she'd gone shopping in Sioux City. I rolled my eyes and tried—only half-successfully—to lay down my judgments.

My family filled the seats: my dad, my grandmother, the clan. In the third act, I delivered Michael's speech to his father like prayer disguised as dialogue. Art held a mirror and asked us both to look. Afterward, Dad slapped his knee, laughing. "If there was anyone to play that part, it was you," he said. I tucked the blessing away where I keep the rare ones.

Exhausted, I napped between shows. When the room went still, a clear desire rose without effort: I wanted to know Lori.

At the cast gathering that night, I asked if she'd be there. Yes. But at the bar she slid in beside a friend and an accidental geometry put me at the far edge of the table. She didn't seem to notice me. I told myself not to care. I cared.

Still, the nudge didn't leave. Now that I knew her name, I called. She said yes to a date.

Walls, Surrender, and a Small Yes

The night of our date, dressed and ready, I hit a wall and confessed it out loud: "I can't do this anymore." Not love as performance. Not games. Not the half-truth dance. I laid down the old storyline in front of God and waited.

There was one theatre in town, and it was showing Cocktail. Freedom looked easy on the screen. Mine would not be. But sitting beside Lori felt steady. After the movie, we found a booth, and the conversation unspooled until the restaurant flipped the lights. Time had slipped; peace had stayed.

At her door, I felt the invitation in the quiet between us. I didn't kiss her. My walls were not all down yet, just lowered enough to see over. But beneath the caution ran a hum I trusted—something gentler than fireworks, stronger than luck. It sounded like timing I didn't have to force.

I knew I'd see her again.

And I did.

Some seasons, God speaks in headlines and deadlines—other times, in cue lines, doorways, and a single bright streak across the night. I learned to listen for all of it—ink on my fingers, script in my hands, a quiet yes in my chest—each a small way of saying: I'm here. Keep going.

Reflections and takeaways

This chapter traces a pivotal season of rooting and reckoning: a drifter-turned-journalist finds belonging in Cherokee, hones a vocation he can trust, experiments with the stage to rediscover voice, and opens—cautiously—to new love: professional integrity, spiritual nudges, and the power of timing braid through each scene.

Core Themes

- Belonging vs. drifting: "I didn't choose Cherokee—Cherokee chose me." The chapter reframes place as calling rather than accident.
- Vocation as service: Journalism becomes a moral practice—standing in tension, reporting with empathy, earning respect quietly.
- Letting go to make room: Releases old relationships and restlessness to receive the right opportunity at the right time.
- Art as mirror: Acting in "Alone Together" surfaces unresolved father-son dynamics—and invites healing.
- Providence and timing: A doorway promotion, a shooting star, a first date's unforced pace—small signs guide big steps.
- Courage to say no: Declining the Atlantic job marks a maturity shift from chasing to discerning.

Character Arc

- From restlessness to rootedness: The move to assistant editor stabilizes career and identity.

- From rebound to readiness: Romance shifts from trying to fill a void to listening for a true connection.
- From proving to receiving: Father's knee-slapping approval lands without striving—and the narrator can hold it.

Key Turning Points

- Controversial budget hearings → cultivates integrity and trust with the community.
- 1988 caucus coverage → expands perspective and professional confidence.
- Doorway promotion → first empowered "no" to a job offer; inner alignment clicks.
- Auditioning for "Alone Together" → returns to creativity, deepens local roots.
- Shooting star on the drive back → symbolic release of the past and opening to new life.
- Final performance with family present → art resolves a private ache (father-son recognition).
- Post-show misfire with Lori → humbling reset that primes a more grounded pursuit.
- First date (Cocktail + long conversation) → connection built on presence, not performance.

Symbols & Motifs

- Shooting star: Grace and permission to move forward.
- Doorways: Unexpected provision; the right door opens without forcing another.

- Stage lights and cue lines: Truth rehearsed safely, then lived bravely.
- Newspaper rhythm (Tue–Sat): A humane cadence that models sustainable calling.

What This Chapter Says About Love

- Love grows in truth-telling spaces—at work, on stage, at a quiet table after a movie.
- Readiness matters: not forcing the kiss signals a shift from hunger to patience.
- Attraction is refined by character—showing up, listening, keeping promises.

What This Chapter Says About Work

- Integrity is attention over time: write with both sides' shoes on.
- Discernment beats hustle: the best opportunities often confirm who you already are.
- Healthy rhythm sustains calling: humane hours make space for community and creativity.

Takeaways You Can Carry Forward

- Practice discernment: When a good door opens, ask if it aligns with who you're becoming—not just what you can achieve.
- Let symbols speak: Note the "shooting stars" in your life—the small but clear consolations that mark transitions.

- Use art to tell the truth: Creative work can metabolize old pain and convert it into growth.
- Choose rootedness: Belonging isn't found; it's formed—through service, collaboration, and consistency.
- Be patient with the heart: Timing is a grace; don't rush what needs to ripen.
- Keep the mirror kind: Accepting unexpected approval (from a parent, a peer, a town) is its own act of courage.

One-Line Essence

A season of saying no to restlessness and yes to providence—where work becomes vocation, art becomes prayer, and love begins with a quiet, unforced yes.

CHAPTER SEVENTEEN
Gifts of Love

"Life is a journey, one that takes us many places and teaches us many things. The lessons we learn on the journey make us who we are."

NISHAN PANWAR

What is true love?

For years, it felt like a riddle I couldn't solve while I navigated my vocation of singleness. I could talk around it, gesture toward it, but define it? No more than I could fully define faith—only live it. And yet, when Lori entered my life, I found myself rising beyond the hopes I'd stored in 1980 and 1984. Something in me—something anchored in God—was changing.

I drifted into the winter of 1988 lighter than I'd felt in years. After the play, after quietly getting to know Lori, after choosing patience over impulse, the world looked different. Love, when it finally arrived, didn't sweep in like a grand overture. It tiptoed in, almost comically, as if it didn't want to startle me.

I was the one ready to settle down. Lori—well, Lori needed convincing.

She'd signed a one-year "contract" with Cherokee. Her new adventure began with a week at the Skyline Inn—not the Holiday Inn by any stretch—and a job as an accountant for the State of Iowa at the massive Cherokee Mental Health Institute. Two bosses quickly became protective mentors, cheering her on as she staked her claim in the world.

After our first date, the Thanksgiving holiday separated us. I drove south to Missouri; she headed east to Atkins, Iowa to see her family. We promised to reconnect at the Cherokee Daily Times Christmas party. I could feel a new current pulling at me, but I fought the urge to rush it. I slowed down. I let the season set the pace. My finances even improved, as if maturity had decided to arrive in more than one area of my life.

Perseverance, after so much stumbling, was finally paying off.

I began to see God's fingerprints on the path that led me to Cherokee. I had answered my call when Mom was diagnosed with cancer and returned home. But for my own sanity, I needed to step out of the caretaker role and into a new life. In that unfamiliar town, God was restoring "the years the locusts had eaten," and with them, my career ambitions.

At the Christmas party, the spark turned into a flame. Lori and I slipped into a rhythm: long talks that went on for hours, simple dinners, shared laughter. Then we parted again—Christmas with our families. Five hours to her parents, four to mine. The miles felt like punctuation marks between sentences we hadn't finished.

After the holidays, another pause crept in. My grandparents, George and Gertrude Wilmes, were celebrating their sixtieth anniversary, and Lori used the weekend to visit her parents. I wondered if another issue was brewing. I carried my questions with me to the church where most of their sixteen children and over eighty grandchildren had gathered. The mural that chronicled our family history stretched across the wall—a living testimony to steady love and stubborn devotion. How had they done it?

The priest began his homily: "We work day by day, week by week, year by year, building toward what we think we want. Then we stop, look around, and realize we've created something different—something far better." His words slid past my defenses and settled in the tender place where hope lives. I wanted that kind of life. I wanted what my grandparents and parents had. And this time, I knew what Lori didn't: our love was real.

Back in Cherokee, love took on a mischievous sense of humor. One morning I arrived at my desk to find a bouquet of roses and a card: "With all my love, Donna Roberts." Ruby Peterson, our grandmotherly Lifestyles Editor, was too good a reporter to ignore a mystery. She peered at the card, gasped, and spent the morning side-eyeing me.

"So," she finally asked, "are those from Lori?"

"Yes," I said, trying not to laugh.

She folded her arms. "Then who is Donna Roberts?"

An inside joke. Lori's alter ego. I let Ruby stew a little longer before admitting as much. The office was still buzzing when it hit me: I'd been "in love" before, but this was different. I started to plan a proposal.

When the moment came, I misread the scene entirely. After dinner at Lori's place, I popped the question. She stood, picked up the dishes, and moved to the sink.

My timing could not have been worse.

She didn't say no. She set a speed limit. We needed to meet each other's families first. She was right—practical where I was impulsive. Opposites do attract, and in our differences, I sensed the future strength of our marriage.

Easter approached. Two weekends, two families, four parents, a crowd of siblings. At some point afterward, I missed the hints she was dropping. She grew uncharacteristically quiet.

"Isn't there something you want to ask me?" she finally blurted.

A light flipped on inside me. I asked again. This time, she said yes.

"Do it the old-fashioned way," she teased. "Ask my father."

I dialed. He answered. I cleared my throat and asked a man I'd met only once for his daughter's hand.

"Well," he stammered, "that's up to the boss." He handed the phone to his wife. We passed the call back to Lori and her mom. We were breaking the mold—talking about a November wedding, a one-year anniversary of that first date. Shell-shocked described her parents. Who was this daughter of theirs, the fiercely independent one, now talking wedding plans?

Soon enough, good news won everyone over. I found myself quietly mourning bachelorhood—the simplicity of being responsible only for yourself. Somewhere in the quiet, I felt my mother's approval. I wished she were still here to share it. I trusted she knew.

In May, we drove through flurries to the Grotto of the Redemption in West Bend for a Catholic Engaged Encounter. The maintenance man hadn't anticipated the cold, and the heat was out. We spent the weekend wrapped in coats, swapping journals back and forth, asking hard questions, revealing who we really were beneath politeness and hope. The six-month marriage prep wasn't hard or overly demanding. It was clarifying. It opened doors we might have left shut: fears, old wounds, dreams we were afraid to speak aloud. The discomfort—both emotional and literal—was a gift.

August brought a different kind of cold. Grandma Tuttle had a mild heart attack. She was 81. Lori and I drove down to St. Francis Hospital in Maryville. Grandma was expectant and peaceful. She told me she looked forward to our November wedding. She let me go, in the most loving way a grandmother can—releasing me to my new life.

She was released later that week. Then came the call. A massive heart attack at home. My grandfather's sister, Mabel, had been there. Everything in me went quiet.

We rushed back for the funeral. When we walked into the house, my grandfather said nothing. He handed me a large scrapbook. Inside, every article I had ever written for the Maryville Daily Forum had been clipped, dated, and pasted with the kind of careful devotion that is its own language of love. I have rarely felt more honored or more known. She had believed in this career before I fully did. I imagined her reunion in heaven—with her children, with my mother. My grandfather and I embraced. Words weren't necessary.

November 11, 1989, arrived like a blessing. Sixty-five degrees in Cherokee. My relatives drove up from Missouri. Lori's came in from Iowa, Chicago, Saint Louis, Maryland. Siblings, cousins, grandparents—the whole, beautiful chaos of two families becoming one.

Earlier that day, I'd given my future father-in-law the key to the basement apartment where they'd be staying. Lori and I had a motel room in town and a flight to California on Monday for the honeymoon. During the reception, he found me in the crowd, beaming.

"I want to be among the first to congratulate you on marrying my daughter," he said, pressing the key into my palm. "And to present you the key to your castle."

The gesture disarmed me. I slid the key into my pocket, proud and humbled all at once.

Later that night, at the apartment door, Lori's mother turned to her husband. "The key?"

He went pale. "I gave it to Marv."

They woke the landlord. Another story for the family vault.

For me, that tiny mishap sealed something sacred between us—a quiet bond with a man of few words who, in one simple moment, welcomed me home.

Love, it turns out, is less a thunderclap and more a series of faithful whispers: a bouquet signed by an inside joke, journal pages in a cold retreat, a priest's homily that names your longing, a scrapbook that proves you were seen, a misplaced key that becomes an emblem. Day by day, week by week, year by year—we build what we think we want, and then God surprises us with something better.

On that warm November day, I knew: this was the life we would build, and it would be far better than anything I had once imagined.

Reflections and Takeaways

This chapter traces a quiet, faithful unfolding of love—not as a thunderclap, but as a series of steady, grace-filled moments. It's a story of maturation: from impulsivity to patience, from caretaker burnout to restored purpose, from solitary striving to the shared rhythm of partnership. Faith anchors the narrative, not as a sermon but as a lived posture—God's providence appears in timing, in mentors, in rituals, and in the way loss and joy braid together.

Two currents run side by side: personal transformation and communal belonging. The homily at the 60th anniversary, the scrapbook from Grandma, the engaged encounter in a chilly retreat center, and the "key to your castle" moment with a father-in-law—each scene affirms that love grows in community and is carried by small, sacramental gestures. Grief (the passing of Grandma Tuttle) doesn't interrupt love's ascent; it deepens it. By the warm November wedding day, love isn't fantasy—it's a practiced promise, shaped by faith, family, and the discipline of listening.

Key Takeaways

- Patience over impulse. True love often requires slowing down, letting timing do its quiet work, and honoring practical steps (meeting families, preparing well).
- Providence in ordinary moments. God's guidance shows up in job moves, mentors, and even "missteps" that become memories.
- Formation through ritual and preparation: The engaged encounter and six-month preparation don't just check boxes; they deepen communication and trust.

- Love and loss can coexist: Grief (Grandma's death) doesn't diminish love's momentum; it dignifies it, linking legacy with new beginnings.
- The power of small gestures: Roses signed "Donna Roberts," a scrapbook of clippings, a misplaced key—tiny acts that carry enormous meaning.
- Complementary strengths: Impulsivity tempered by practicality becomes a shared wisdom—the engine of a resilient marriage.
- Identity affirmed through relationship: The grandmother's scrapbook validates vocation and voice; being seen fuels becoming.

Memorable Symbols & What They Mean

- The family mural: Legacy, endurance, and the long view of love.
- The priest's homily: Building a life that turns out "different and far better" than intended.
- The "Donna Roberts" roses: Intimacy, playfulness, inside language of love.
- The scrapbook: Being known and celebrated—love as witness to one's calling.
- The key to the "castle": Welcome, belonging, and the humility that bonds families.

Reflection Prompts

- Where have you seen "restoration of the years the locusts have eaten" in your life?

- Which small gestures have meant the most in your relationships? Why?
- Are you more impulsive or cautious in love? How could you practice complementary virtues?
- How do you invite faith into everyday relationship decisions (timing, family, preparation)?
- What legacies from your family do you want to carry forward—or gently revise?

Practical Applications

- Schedule a "slow conversation" date: No agenda, just curiosity—ask and answer one deep question each.
- Create a shared ritual: Journal letters to each other during big transitions (engagement, moves, grief).
- Meet the village: Intentionally engage mentors, siblings, and parents—build the network that will support your commitment.
- Name your opposite strengths: List one way your differences make you stronger; practice gratitude for it this week.
- Honor legacy: Preserve a keepsake (photos, letters, clippings) that affirms identity and reminds you who's cheering you on.

Lines to Carry Forward

- Love often arrives as faithful whispers, not fanfare.
- Day by day, God surprises us with something better than what we planned.

- Preparation isn't a hurdle—it's a gift that opens deeper trust.
- Grief can be a companion on the road to joy, not a detour from it.

This chapter reveals love as a patient, faith-guided construction—built from small, tender acts, tempered by loss, strengthened by community, and ultimately, far better than the plans we first imagined.

CHAPTER EIGHTEEN

Rising Beyond Hope

Grief is a curious companion. It wraps around us in different ways, shaping our thoughts and actions in ways we often don't understand. After losing my mother, I drifted through the following year, immersing myself in my new role as a radio disc jockey in Atchison, Kansas. Looking back, I realize I was in shock, numbed by the whirlwind of events in 1984.

The Ripple Effect of Loss

Her passing didn't just leave a void in my heart; it sent ripples through my entire family. In my twenties, I sought independence by joining the military and exploring diverse cultures across the West Coast, East Coast, Hawaii, Japan, and the Philippines. Throughout those years, my mother kept me tethered to home with her weekly letters, her words bridging the distance and grounding me in my roots. It was through those exchanges that I unearthed my creative spirit—a blessing that often felt like a curse.

In 1985, I found solace in the local community theater in Atchison, stepping into the role of a Thespian. Reconnecting with a college friend, I was cast in three plays, each role more demanding than the last. It was my escape, a way to numb the unbearable pain of loss. There were countless moments when exciting news would bubble up inside me, only to be crushed by the stark reminder that I could no longer share it with my mother. The sting of that realization was surreal and haunting.

My faith in God and the Catholic Church deepened during this turbulent time, yet I felt like a wanderer in a life that had lost its map. The absence of a grief support group in Atchison left me adrift, chasing fleeting illusions of love and happiness.

An unexpected twist occurred during my first two months in Atchison. My novel's storyline had come to a standstill when my mother's health declined. A paralyzing writer's block gripped me, my manuscript tucked away in a briefcase as I shuffled between my part-time job and the empty pages of my life. In those quiet moments, I began journaling—pouring my heart into letters that would never be sent. It was a cathartic release, a way to process my grief.

When I finally unearthed my manuscript, I felt a spark reignite. Words flowed freely, and within weeks, I completed the rough draft of *The Golden Key*. It became my lifeline—a dream that kept me buoyed amidst the storm. Yet, as time marched on, I had to confront the reality that this dream might never manifest as I had envisioned.

A New Chapter

The journey of writing *The Golden Key* was transformative. My obsession with becoming a published author consumed me, but eventually, life took precedence. I relegated that manuscript to the depths of a drawer, overshadowed by the responsibilities of my newspaper career and married life. But I knew there was another story waiting to be told.

In 2015, I published the first edition of this book, titled *Beyond the Horizon*. It became a living tribute to my mother, a testament to our family's journey through the valley of grief. One truth emerged: life would never be the same for any of us.

Lessons from the Journey

As I reflect on the adventures and lessons that lay ahead, I realize we often discover our true selves through the fires of adversity. A knight may wear shiny armor, but the real testament to their strength lies in the dings and dents they bear from battle.

There is a profound purpose in sharing my stories. I intend to inspire hope and instill a belief that a higher power watches over us. This life is indeed a test of our resilience. We will stumble, we will falter, but there is a divine desire for our best.

My mother was a humble woman, giving selflessly to her family, her church, and her community. She embraced life fully, blooming like a flower in a desert.

As 1985 unfolded, I turned the page to new chapters in my life, with my mother's memory guiding me. My faith in Christ fortified my perseverance on this journey. I knew God recognized my sacrifices, and I was destined for even more dramatic changes in the years ahead.

In Cherokee, I found stability in my career and met my soulmate, Lori, who would walk beside me on this path.

Reflections and Takeaways

Quick Snapshot

- A tender, reflective hinge chapter moving from numb grief to purposeful living.
- Creativity (radio, theater, journaling, novel-writing) and faith become lifelines.
- The dream of publication evolves into a tribute and a deeper vocation; love and stability emerge (Cherokee, Lori).

Core Themes

- Grief as a shaper, not just a wound.
- Creativity as catharsis: journaling and theater as safe containers for pain.
- Faith as a compass when life "loses its map."
- Maternal legacy: letters as tether, memory as guide.
- Acceptance over fixation: allowing dreams to change form.
- Community and isolation coexisting (no grief group; church and theater fill gaps).
- Resilience: strength shown in "dings and dents," not shine.

Emotional Arc

- Shock and drift → ache of absence → solace in performance → catharsis in journaling → rekindled agency (finishing The Golden Key) → acceptance and reorientation → tribute and testimony → readiness for love and stability.

Symbols & Motifs

- The briefcase/manuscript: dormant self awaiting rebirth.
- Letters: bridges between distance and home.
- Stage/masks: experimenting with identities to survive pain.
- Knight's dents: honored scars as credentials.
- Desert flower: the mother's resilient spirit.
- "The Golden Key": unlocking selfhood and purpose.

What Shifts Here

- From chasing publication to sharing testimony as service (2015 edition).
- From wandering to rootedness (career in Cherokee; meeting Lori).
- From hope as wishful thinking to hope as practiced faith and action.

Life Takeaways for Readers

- It's okay to shelve a dream; its meaning can mature with you.
- Journaling can be a private sanctuary when community support is scarce.
- Art and faith are complementary paths through grief.
- Scars don't disqualify us—they credential us.
- Love after loss doesn't replace; it accompanies.

Micro-Practices

- Write a letter you'll never send to the person you lost.
- "Briefcase check": list dormant projects and revisit quarterly.
- Choose a symbol of your loved one's legacy for your workspace.
- 10-minute read-aloud (psalm, monologue, prayer) to move emotion through the body.
- Monthly service act in their honor.

Journal prompts

- What does "beyond hope" mean here—how is it different from waiting or wishing?
- Which creative practice feels most healing, and why?
- What family rituals shape your identity and endurance?
- What dream have you set aside—and what form might it take now?
- Has your faith ever become a map in the absence of a map?

Memorable Insights (Distilled)

- Real strength shows in the dents, not the shine.
- Letters can bridge miles—and years.
- A project or a dream can be a lifeline even if it never becomes reality.
- Blooming in a desert is possible with the right roots.
- Dreams can change shape without dying.

In Closing

- A moving transitional chapter that reframes grief as guidance, aligns ambition with devotion, and opens the door to covenantal love and steadier ground.

Author's Note

The next chapter of my story awaits in the second book of the *Odyssey of Hope* series. I invite you to dive into *Chronicles of Hope: Persevering Faith*. Additionally, *A Quest for Freedom: A Golden Key Novel* is available on Amazon in various formats and Book Baby Bookshop in paperback.

If you found meaning in *Rising Beyond Hope*, I would be grateful for your Amazon review. Your feedback highlights this series, which I see as a tool for evangelization and a means of assisting others in navigating their grief and overcoming life's challenges. I want to remind them that hope exists, and they are never alone.

Jesus is in the boat with us! All we need to do is step in and ask Him to guide us where He wills. I assure you, as He promised me, it will be a wild and transformative ride.

To stay updated on the *Odyssey of Hope* series, follow my blog and sign up for my newsletter at www.marvinwilmes.com.

Facebook: https://www.facebook.com/keypublications

Instagram: https://www.instagram.com/mlwilmes/

Email: odysseyofhope@gmail.com

www.ingramcontent.com/pod-product-compliance
Lightning Source LLC
LaVergne TN
LVHW090605110826
845146LV00001B/267

* 9 7 9 8 9 8 9 1 6 1 3 1 7 *